# SPEAK
# WELSH
## outside class

*This book is dedicated to the memory of
Florence Elmer who encouraged me to keep writing.*

# SPEAK WELSH

## outside class

### YOU CAN DO IT!

DR LYNDA PRITCHARD NEWCOMBE

First impression: 2016
© Lynda Pritchard Newcombe & Y Lolfa Cyf., 2016

Cover design: Y Lolfa

ISBN:  978 1 78461 273 3

Published and printed in Wales
on paper from well-maintained forests by
Y Lolfa Cyf., Talybont, Ceredigion SY24 5HE
e-mail  ylolfa@ylolfa.com
website  www.ylolfa.com
tel  01970 832 304
fax  832 782

# Contents

# Foreword

We share a love for Welsh and want to do our bit to ensure it remains a living language. Of course, our relationships with Welsh – and our motives for learning it – are very varied. In my case, I grew up hearing conversations between my mother and grandfather and singing Welsh hymns in chapel. In school I had to choose between Welsh and French and opted for French. I was left with a good passive knowledge of Welsh but a feeling of deep loss.

Living outside Wales as an adult, my opportunities for taking things further were limited. I was finally jerked out of my inertia when I enrolled on the Open University distance learning *Croeso* course where Lynda was a tutor. There I was able to benefit from her many years of experience with adults at all levels and to start filling in the holes in my knowledge of the language.

Your story may be similar or completely different. But what all of

Professor Viv Edwards speaking at the Melbourne Convention Exhibition Centre.
Photo: Viv Edwards

us encounter as adult learners is the difficulty in what is often called 'crossing the bridge' to fluency in Welsh, something which can only be achieved by stepping outside the safe confines of the classroom into the real world. It takes courage – the courage to make mistakes, to seem foolish, and to persevere when the person you are talking to is either irritated by the artificiality of conducting a conversation which would be much easier in English or thinks that they are helping by switching languages.

This is where this eminently practical and user-friendly book comes into its own. In it Lynda shares her understanding of the confidence issues for learners both in and outside the classroom, and offers strategies for moving forward. It leaves you feeling that you are not alone, that *you can do it!*

Viv Edwards
Professor of Language in Education
University of Reading

# Introduction

You've been learning Welsh for some time and getting on well. But when someone talks to you outside class you freeze and your mind goes blank. Other times you pluck up the courage to say something in Welsh and the Welsh speaker speaks English!

Don't give up! You may even be talking too 'posh'. Ever thought of that?

Learning Welsh is one thing. Using it is another. Many learners do really well in the classroom but give up when trying to speak 'in the real world'. They find it too challenging. Follow the advice in this book and it won't happen to you!

With my tips on learning Welsh, you will see your confidence grow. Language learning is different from most other learning. It's so public to put into practice what you have learned in class. You put yourself on the line and feel exposed and sensitive.

If someone ignores you or laughs at you do not assume that they think you are hopeless. They may feel awkward with learners or they may just be having a bad day. They may feel your Welsh is 'too correct'. They may speak *iaith yr aelwyd* – the language of the hearth – and have never learned Welsh at school. Please don't take it to heart. Try to look at it from their point of view.

This book offers practical advice on remembering vocabulary, sharpening up pronunciation, coping with native speakers, building confidence, dealing with discouragement, time management and much more.

You may only want to get by in Welsh – chat with friends at the rugby club or speak to parents at your children's school. This book will help you achieve your goal.

When we learn to play a musical instrument or train for a sport we do not reach a high standard instantly, but over time our skills develop. It is the same with speaking a language.

En route to our main goal we achieve targets that keep us motivated. I would like to be fluent in French and Spanish but for now I am content to book tickets, go shopping, ask directions and order meals. In fact I get quite a buzz when a French or Spanish person is willing to speak to me without resorting to English!

There will be many 'snakes and ladders' experiences, but with perseverance you will reach your targets.

Tori James, the first Welsh woman to climb Everest, was inspired by her grandmother's words when she was child: 'There's no such word as can't.' Tori tells her story in *Peak Performance*, an inspiring *quick read* book. Tori says:

> If you can tell yourself you can do something, you will... If you really want to achieve something, it's a question of starting small, creating building blocks, and putting them together in the right order. It's all very well saying, 'I'd like to be able to run a marathon in a year's time,' but if you do nothing for the first six months, your chances are going to be pretty slim. You need to have a plan and be realistic. But more than anything, you need to have a vision to see yourself achieving your goal and should never give up, even when the going gets tough.

This book will not disappoint those whose ultimate goal is to speak Welsh or those who wish just to get by in some situations. It does not promise that everything will be easy or speedy but it does encourage and provide a wealth of practical advice and tips. I am fluent in Welsh, speak German quite well and am able to get by in several other languages... it wasn't always easy but I did it. You can too!

I learned the piano as a child and, unlike many, I still play, though mainly for my own amusement. I would have liked to learn a woodwind instrument at school. Circumstances made that impossible.

So I often said over the years, 'I'd love to play the clarinet.' But I never did anything about it. Shortly before he died my father said to me, 'Why are you always saying that? Why don't you just do it?' A few months later I bought a clarinet at the age of 42 and started learning. I do not aspire to play in the Albert Hall but I have achieved my goal. I am able to play pieces such as 'The Swan' which gives me great pleasure, as well as duets with my husband accompanying me on the piano. I even played in a scratch band on Level 3 of St David's Hall in Cardiff once. Terrifying and terrific!

If we want something enough we can make it happen.

So... over to you!

## Some Basics for Starters

| Bore da | Boreh da | Good morning |
|---|---|---|
| Shwmae | Shoomahee | Hello/Hi |
| Diolch | Deeolch | Thank you |
| Hwyl! | Hooeel | Good bye |
| Nos da | Nohs da | Goodnight |
| Pen-blwydd Hapus | Pehn blooeth hapis | Happy Birthday |
| Nadolig Llawen | Nadolig llahooehn | Merry Christmas |

Read Tori's inspiring story in *Peak Performance* by Tori James (Accent Press, 2013).

# Chapter 1

# Using what you know

Many learners have told me they cope perfectly well in class and have even passed examinations in Welsh but panic when faced with a native speaker.

Often what we lack is not ability but self-belief. This book is about building up confidence to use in the community the Welsh you have been learning in class. We'll look at what hinders learners from speaking. We'll find ways of overcoming these issues.

'When I see her, I cross the street,' one Welsh learner admitted in a focus group discussion. Other students admitted they also found ways of avoiding Welsh speakers. Yet at the same time they wanted to practise and felt disappointed they had not taken the opportunity.

Revolutionary changes in methods and use of day-to-day language in class have made Welsh, since the 1960s, a more attractive and fashionable language for adults to learn, and registrations on Welsh for Adults classes have soared. Approximately 15,000 students most years are attending Welsh for Adults classes at a variety of levels. Others are learning on-line, with private companies, and informally with friends and family. There are many learners outside Wales too, in particular in London, *Y Wladfa* (the Welsh settlement in Patagonia) and the USA.

The previously widely held view that Welsh was so difficult it could only be learned in childhood or not at all, is disappearing. Learners from as far afield as Japan, the USA, Australia, Iran and Bangladesh are becoming fluent speakers. Yet despite the escalating numbers taking up the challenge, not all learners achieve the level to which they aspire. Why?

Akiko, a fluent learner from Japan, with learners from her summer course.
Photo: Akiko Matsuyama

There is, of course, a high drop-out rate in all areas of adult learning. There are many reasons. Personal circumstances such as bereavement, divorce and family illness can make it difficult to keep up. Emergencies can also sap your energy. If the roof leaked or the pipes burst when we were children, we just carried on reading the *Bunty* or *Beano* while the adults in our lives sorted it all out. Adults wanting to learn another language and leading busy lives clearly need to be disciplined with their time.

There are also other stumbling blocks, the course book, the tutor, the methods used in class, the student group, the venue... you may dislike all or some of them, and give up. But lack of confidence is probably the biggest issue for language learners discouraged by the very public nature of speaking in a second language. Anxiety spoils performance, especially if you don't feel supported in the community.

Many complain it is difficult to persuade native speakers to hold a conversation with learners. 'Welsh speakers don't want us as part of their group,' some learners have said. Others, 'They don't want us to join their club.'

This criticism, of course, is not limited to Welsh speakers, and in later chapters I will be giving examples of learners of other languages. Where there is a common language, such as English, there is temptation for both learners and native speakers to use it to make life easier. This is clearly the case in Wales where determination to practise the language is particularly important.

Using a second language outside the classroom, though satisfying, can be a serious challenge for adults. Sadly there's no quick fix for fluency – but many ways to make the process smoother and more enjoyable. But rather than wasting energy on the blaming game, it's much more helpful to search for solutions. There are many ways of learning to 'get by' and we will look at these.

**You will find tips in the chapters which follow on:**
- improving pronunciation
- building up your vocabulary
- how to react when Welsh speakers speak too quickly, use dialect, idioms and slang or turn to English
- developing strategies for practising with family and friends
- finding Welsh speakers willing to help you
- gaining in confidence
- carrying on learning when life is pressurised
- imbibing the culture
- making the best use of the internet, media, books and magazines.

I have taught adult language classes for over thirty years, been involved in research on bilingualism, and written books and articles on the topic. But, as well as my voice, you will hear the voices of successful language learners and tutors from Wales and beyond. All have useful advice to impart and interesting stories to tell. By the end of the book the aim is for you to be chatting away in Welsh to that person you avoided!

# Top Tip and Task

Before we move on I want you to make a decision.
Make the following phrases part of you. Say them over
and over until you know you will never forget them:

### *Dw i'n dysgu Cymraeg*
(Doo een dusgi Comeraig)
I'm learning Welsh

### *Siaradwch yn araf, os gwelwch chi'n dda*
(Sharadooch un arav, oss gooelooch een dda)
Speak slowly, please

### *Eto, os gwelwch chi'n dda*
(Eto, oss gooelooch een dda)
Again, please

OK, if you are just starting don't worry too much about
*os gwelwch chi'n dda.* It is quite a mouthful to begin with.
Just use the word – *plîs* (pleez). Many fluent speakers do that.

Lesson 1 in the BBC Catchphrase series will help you to pronounce Welsh:
http://www.bbc.co.uk/wales/catchphrase/catchphrase1/

Go back to the expressions at the end of the introductory chapter and
make sure you know them too and are confident saying them aloud.

No excuses. There's pronunciation advice in the book and online and I
also suggest trying to find a Welsh speaker who might help you –
someone at your work, a neighbour, a friend or a friend of a friend.

Many people enjoy being asked for their help – but don't make
unrealistic demands; even a half-hour a week face to face, or just
five minutes twice a week on the phone will help.

**When the above phrases are second nature to you then –
and only then! – move on to Chapter 2.**

**Chapter 2**

# How do you say that?
# Pronunciation

## Why is it important?

Think of how a Welsh speaker will feel if they have to strain to understand what you say even though you are using the correct words and phrases. Do you know people who are learning English? Who are the easiest ones to chat to – those who have perfect grammar but poor pronunciation or those who make grammatical errors but have excellent pronunciation? No prizes for guessing. It's pronunciation, of course!

A friend of ours who is learning English has come out with gems such as, 'I have broken the thumb on my left foot.' As this is delivered with perfect English pronunciation, chatting is fun. On the other hand, we have met second-language English speakers who speak more accurately but their poor pronunciation leaves us reaching for Nurofen!

Learners and tutors are aware that speaking a new language can bring on discouragement and fatigue. However, there is little awareness of first-language speaker weariness when trying to help learners. When Derek, a learner of German, Russian and Finnish, was interviewed by a world expert on language learning, Earl Stevick, he stressed that this may well have been the case, particularly if it was difficult for the first-language speaker to follow the learner's accent:

> As you go from one language to another, the sheer exhaustion that follows the first time you use the language in a social evening is hard to describe! And it works in the other direction also. I think we leave the first-language speakers as worn out as we are... When I am learning a new language, I try to have just as little foreign accent as possible... I have found in dealing with foreigners that their knowledge of grammar and vocabulary didn't make a big difference. The heavier their accent the less they were understood. So I have concluded that for me, learning pronunciation is just as important as learning grammar, if not more so.

Pronunciation is more important therefore than grammar and certainly more important than the infamous Welsh mutations. Many Welsh speakers are not too hot on those! So make pronunciation central in your learning plan. Do not worry too much about grammar in the early days of learning. That will follow.

It is rare for second-language speakers to lose their accents completely, but if they work on pronunciation from the beginning they should make themselves more than acceptable to Welsh speakers. Jen Llywelyn, author of *Welsh in a Year* offers wise advice: 'WORK ON PRONUNCIATION FROM THE START! Everything depends on it! Be prepared to feel silly, but do it, get it right, and you will find everything is easier, and what's more, people will understand you!'

Listening, of course, is a non-threatening way of familiarising yourself with Welsh sounds and laying the foundation for good pronunciation. Decide that you are going to listen to some Welsh every day from now on, even if it is only for five minutes.

When faced with written Welsh for the first time, learners from outside Wales have been known to exclaim, 'There aren't any vowels!' Richard Stilgoe, on the TV programme *Countdown* some years ago, commented on the word *cynhyrchydd* (producer) saying he did not know that words could exist without vowels. Of course, the answer is simple.

'Y' is a vowel in Welsh.

Now *cynhyrchydd*, pronounced *cinhurchidd*, is not the ideal first word to learn! 'Y' is the only inconsistent letter with several ways of pronouncing it. However, that's the bad news over. The good news is that when you have learned how to pronounce all the other letters in the Welsh alphabet, that's it. They obey the rules. How easy is that!

Remember how hard it is for English learners from overseas. As well as the oft-quoted cough, bough, plough, though, dough, trough etc., there are myriads of ways of pronouncing words that look as though they should follow a simple pattern.

Welsh spelling is very regular. I have provided English equivalent pronunciations for Welsh words used in the book. I have listed the main letters and letter combinations that I have noticed trip learners up, particularly learners from outside Wales.

| PRONUNCIATION/YNGANU | |
|---|---|
| *dd* as in *dydd* (day) | As the 'th' in the English word 'that' |
| *th* as in *gwaith* (work) | As the 'th' in the English word 'thanks' |
| *ll* as in *llaw* (hand) | Put the tip of the tongue just behind the top teeth and breathe out |
| *ng* as in *rhwng* (between) | As in the English word 'gang' |
| *f* as in *rhif* (number) | As a 'v' in the English word 'vase' |
| *ff* as in *ffa* (beans) | As an 'f' in the English word 'fox' |
| *r* as in *car* (car) | It is very important to roll the 'r' in Welsh in order to sound natural. Think of the English word 'tariff'. Learners tend to forget to do so, particularly at the end of words such as *amser* (time), *car* (car). |

| | |
|---|---|
| *ei* and *eu* as in *eithaf* (quite) and *teulu* (family) | As in the English word *way* |
| *aw* as in llawn (full) | Like the *ou* in the English word *cloud* |
| *wy* as in *pwy* (who) | Think of the English word 'gooey', remove the 'g' and say 'ooey' quickly |
| *yw* as in *byw* (to live) | Rhymes with 'eue' in the English word 'queue' |
| *c* is always hard as in English 'cat'. Never soft as in the English 'cease' | Examples: *cath* – cat<br>*cariad* – love, boyfriend, girlfriend<br>*canu* – to sing |
| *o* as in *glo* (coal) | It is difficult to find a similar sound in English but it is definitely not as in 'dough' but more like the 'oo' in the English word 'door' |
| *e* as in *ble* (where) | Another letter where it is difficult to find the equivalent sound in English. It is similar to the French word for 'tea' (té) |
| *u* as in *du* (black) | As 'ee' in the English word 'bee' |
| *y* as in *dyn* ('man')<br>*y* as in *llyn* ('lake')<br>*y* also as in *Cymru* (Wales) | As 'ee' in the English word 'deep'<br>As 'i' in the English word 'tin'<br>As 'u' in the English word 'up' |

Practise these sounds with first-language speakers or fluent learners, in particular the vowels 'o' and 'e' and rolled 'r' and listen carefully to CDs/MP3s and the media. There are two types of listening – active and passive. Active listening is when the learner concentrates on the language. Passive listening is listening to something in the background. It will help learners imbibe pronunciation with no effort. When performing tedious tasks such as ironing, defrosting the freezer or weeding the vegetable patch, listening to Radio Cymru or Welsh songs will help. In fact I always tell beginners to listen to Radio

Cymru for at least five minutes a day to become familiar with the sounds even though they will understand very little. This could be in the car or on a smartphone.

Closely linked with pronunciation is stress. But there is no need to get stressed about stress. In Welsh it is very simple: just stress the second-to-last syllable. This rule is preserved even in the anglicised versions of many Welsh names, such as Car**MAR**then, and in personal names such as Rhi**ANN**on. So if you were talking about television in Welsh you would say *telEdu*, and Christmas is *NadOLig*. There are very few exceptions to this rule. You can learn these later on.

Recent years have witnessed a recognition among providers and tutors that gaining competence in rhythm and stress is essential if learners are to communicate with *Cymry Cymraeg* (Welsh-speaking Welsh people) with ease. Research is on-going at Bangor University and the results will be fed into the methodology used in the teaching of *Cymraeg i Oedolion* (Welsh for Adults).

This is not an issue exclusive to Wales. Putting stress in the right place makes all language learners sound more native-like and may prevent misunderstandings. I have heard the iconic language tutor, Michel Thomas, stop his Spanish students and say, 'If you say it like that you will not be understood' when they placed stress on the wrong syllable. Again, passive as well as active listening will help.

Daoudi, a Farsi learner in Iran, found he was making sounds that were totally incomprehensible to the locals. Then he tried to pick up the rhythm of the language and, as soon as he started speaking Farsi in the local rhythm, he was understood, even though sometimes his vowels and consonants were a little different from theirs. He also noticed that, despite his limited Farsi vocabulary, his speech was more accepted than the speech of several other people from his part of the world who had wider vocabularies than he.

*Goslef* (intonation) is very important to first-language Welsh speakers, though most of them do not realise this. Sometimes Welsh speakers have commented to me about learners, 'S/he does not sound like a learner.' Often such learners make many grammar and mutation errors but their intonation makes them sound so authentic that the Welsh speaker has not even noticed. Latching on to the rhythm of the language then makes learners more appealing to Welsh speakers.

The singer and presenter Wynne Evans (Yes, Gio Compario from the GoCompare.com TV ads!) started learning Welsh on *cariad@iaith* (love4language). He was filmed with other celebrities learning Welsh for a week. Wynne has limited time for classes and study because of his heavy work schedule, yet his Welsh flows beautifully. I heard Betsan Powys interview him at *Y Mochyn Du*, a pub restaurant in Cardiff as part of the festival, *Tafwyl*. The session was very enjoyable and the learners present were given a boost. Yes, he made several grammar and mutation errors and sometimes asked *'Beth yw'r gair am...?'* ('What's the word for...') but no one really cared as he communicated so well. In his Christmas Day show no one would have realised Wynne was a learner if he hadn't dropped it into a conversation. His programmes on S4C are well worth watching. Use subtitles if you are just starting to learn Welsh.

The singer and presenter, Wynne Evans, a learner who communicates well in Welsh.
Photo: Wynne Evans

The opera singer, Gabriel Wyner, author of *Fluent Forever – How to learn any language fast and never forget it*, believes learning pronunciation first is the key to success in learning to speak any language. According to Gabriel, singers learn the pronunciation of languages first because they need to sing in these languages long before they have time to learn to communicate in them. While mastering the sounds, their ears become attuned to them, making vocabulary and speaking skills develop more quickly. 'While we're at it, we pick up a snazzy, accurate accent,' adds Gabriel. Is this why Wynne's pronunciation and intonation is so good?

I use the CD *Dewis o Ddwsin i Ddysgwyr* with students. It contains twelve songs including the Welsh national anthem '*Hen Wlad fy Nhadau*' (Land of my Fathers), and traditional songs such as '*Ar Lan y Môr*' (Down by the Sea) and '*Calon Lân*' (A Pure Heart), as well as songs to help students learn the days of the week, months of the year, parts of the body and weather vocabulary, as well as pronunciation advice. There is an accompanying booklet. There are twelve tracks *cyfeiliant yn unig* (accompaniment only) so learners can have a go at *caraocê* (karaoke). Great fun! Students have told me that they find that Bryn Fôn and Trebor Edwards enunciate clearly when singing and are easy to follow.

Pronunciation and intonation certainly need a more prominent place in all language learning programmes. They make or break a learner and are often not emphasised enough in the early days of learning. I know learners who have a very wide vocabulary and a very sound mastery of grammar, yet Welsh speakers and other learners tend to give them a wide berth. Why? They are so hard to understand. Their conversation does not flow and strains the listeners' ears. Reader – however good you are at grammar and mutations and however much vocabulary you know, if your pronunciation is weak and you don't have the rhythm, go back to basics and learn to apply the pronunciation rules. Listen to as much Welsh as possible until you get into the rhythm and find a Welsh speaker to correct any errors. Otherwise, you will be like someone putting beautiful plants into a garden before taking out the weeds and turning over the ground. The plants will not flourish.

The pioneering Welsh tutor, Gwilym Roberts, emphasises reading aloud to help build confidence using language and foster good pronunciation and intonation. Do this as often as you can. In the early stages bite-size is best. Gwilym stresses perfecting 'o' ('oh' not 'ow') and 'e' ('bleh' not 'blay') at the end of words, as pronouncing these in an English way may grate on first-language speakers! If possible record yourself and ask Welsh speakers and / or your tutor to listen to you and correct any blemishes. Keep recording till they are hard-pressed to find any issues.

## Want to find out more?

Heini Gruffudd, *Live Welsh* (Y Lolfa, 2012).

Jen Llywelyn, *Welsh in a Year* (Y Lolfa, 2009).

Lynda Pritchard Newcombe, *Think without Limits: You CAN speak Welsh* (Gwasg Carreg Gwalch, 2009).

Christine Jones, *Teach Yourself Welsh Grammar* (Chapter 1), (Hodder Headline, 2007).

Edwin Lewis, *Teach Yourself Welsh Dictionary* (pp.349–50), (Hodder Headline, 2003).

Gabriel Wyner, *Fluent Forever – How to learn any language fast and never forget it* (Harmony, 2014).

David and Amelia Hedley Williams, *Dewis o Ddwsin i Ddysgwyr* (CD and booklet, available by e-mailing daihedley@hotmail.co.uk or phoning 07940275896).

Michel Thomas, *Spanish Foundation Course* (CDs and booklet), (Hodder & Stoughton, 2011).

**Chapter 3**

# So many words!

## Vocabulary

One of the reasons language learners give up is anxiety and lack of confidence – key issues in learning anything at all and crucial for using what you have learned. We will be discussing these issues in more detail later.

Lack of confidence and anxiety impair language learning. In this chapter we look at ways of building up a reservoir of words to aid communication and boost learners' self-belief. You may be surprised to learn that even if you are a complete beginner you already know many Welsh words. Why is this? Like other European languages, Welsh uses many international words and has some borrowings from other languages. Some of these may be spelt or pronounced slightly differently to English but you will recognise them. Heini Gruffudd lists over a hundred of these words in his helpful book, *Live Welsh*.

Below are some you might find useful:

| | |
|---|---|
| Banc | Bank |
| Beic | Bike |
| Car (roll the 'r' in Welsh) | Car |
| Cloc | Clock |
| Copi | Copy |
| Criced (kriked) | Cricket |
| Drama | Drama |
| Gêm (gehm) | Game |
| Fflat | Flat |

| | |
|---|---|
| Ffliw | Flu |
| Ffôn (phohn) | Phone |
| Ham | Ham |
| Inc | Ink |
| Jam | Jam |
| Lager (roll the 'r' in Welsh) | Lager |
| Lamp | Lamp |
| Lwc (look) | Luck |
| Map | Map |
| Parc | Park |
| Parti | Party |
| Poced | Pocket |
| Potel | Bottle |
| Rygbi | Rugby |
| Radio | Radio |
| Sbectol | Spectacles |
| Sgandal | Scandal |
| Sgarff | Scarf |
| Siampŵ | Shampoo |
| Siop | Shop |
| Stori | Story |
| Tacsi | Taxi |

Now, isn't that encouraging? So you are not starting completely from scratch.

What else can we do to boost your confidence?

*New York Times* best-selling author, Tim Ferriss, recommends selecting the subject matter you wish to speak about in the early stages of learning and concentrate on the relevant vocabulary – and just that. Practise these topics with your tutor and others. Have questions ready for Welsh speakers. If you know they enjoy rugby, have ready, *'Welaist ti'r gêm ddydd Sadwrn?'* ('Did you see the game on Saturday?'). Even learn a few adjectives to describe the match – *gwych* (excellent), *anhygoel* (incredible) and *siomedig* (disappointing).

Build up a vocabulary on topics of interest to you and your contacts. If sport isn't your thing but socialising and eating out is, there is no point in spending ages on learning words such as *bachwr* (hooker)! Learn words for food, drink, cutlery and crockery: fish and chips for instance is *pysgod a sglodion.* Learn words that are close to English, such as *sinema.* Here's an example of starter words for socialising from Steve Morris and Paul Meara of Swansea University.

| 1 | TAFARN (tavarn) | pub |
|---|---|---|
| 2 | SINEMA | cinema |
| 3 | TŶ BWYTA (tee booeeta) | restaurant |
| 4 | THEATR (theahtr) | theatre |
| 5 | BWYTA (booeeta) | to eat |
| 6 | MWYNHAU (mooeenhay) | to enjoy |
| 7 | MYND* (mihnd) | to go |
| 8 | YFED (uhvehd) | to drink |
| 9 | PRYD O FWYD (preed o vooed) | meal |
| 10 | FFRIND (frind) | friend |

\* -*mynd am dro* **(go for a walk)** / *mynd â* **(to take)** / *mynd â'r ci am dro...* **(take the dog for a walk)** + *mynd dros ben llestri* **(go over the top)**

Learn some of these words today and make them a part of you. Steve and Paul have written a book in north and south Walian versions of core vocabulary, with phrases for beginners. The book includes a short chapter by Paul, a world expert on acquiring vocabulary, with his tips for learning words.

You can approach learning vocabulary in a number of ways. Benny Lewis, fluent in ten languages and with a smattering of over twenty, stresses that it's good to learn phrases or even sentences rather than words in isolation, particularly if you are aiming for fluency. Rather than learn the words *bwyta* and *mynd* for 'to eat' and 'to go', learn *Dw i'n hoffi bwyta siocled* (I like eating chocolate) and *Dw i'n mynd i'r sinema heno* (I am going to the cinema tonight).

Some people actually enjoy sitting down to learn lists, others prefer flash cards, others use link words and some like to get native speakers to record words and phrases so that they are able to listen and repeat them over and over.

Whatever method you choose, I would recommend having a small notebook – A5 or even smaller – with you at all times. Note down all new words and phrases from class and those you come across in the community. Take the book everywhere you go so that you can look at it at odd moments, such as when hanging around for public transport, waiting for a medical appointment, even queuing in a shop. Little and often is best. Look at one page of your notebook before you fall asleep at night and revise the same page first thing in the morning.

- **Consider keeping a vocabulary book divided into categories.** Use the second half of your notebook and divide it up under headings such as *anifeiliaid* (animals), *bwyd* (food), *chwaraeon* (games). Choose topics that are of use in your particular settings. It depends on your level how much you will include. Under *anifeiliaid*, for instance, a beginner could include just the animal names, such as *ci* (dog), *cath* (cat), *cwningen* (rabbit), but leave space for later on when you can put the icing on the cake with words such as *canu grwndi* (to purr), *anwesu* (to stroke) and *llety cathod* (cattery).

- **Some people find making flash cards, either hard copies or electronic, very useful.** Again it is a good idea to look at these before sleeping and first thing the following morning. Take some cards out with you every day so that you can look at them regularly. Find a fluent speaker or advanced learner to repeat the Welsh words to you and test you. To make the flash cards more exciting you could use your photographs and write the Welsh word on the back, cut out photos from magazines or even a printout from Google images. Using images with the Welsh word will help you to think in Welsh.

- **The link word series has proved popular with language learners over many years.** How do link words work? An example in Welsh would be the word *ci* (dog) which is pronounced as the English word 'key'. You visualise a dog with a key in its mouth to help you remember the word for dog: *ci* sounds like the English word 'key'. It is well worth giving link words a try as many have learnt successfully following this method.

- **Put post-it notes around the house.** This is particularly useful if learning with young children.

- **For numbers keep throwing one or two dice until the numbers become second nature.** Then add more dice and practise adding and subtracting. It is possible to buy dice that go up to twenty.

Whatever method or methods you use, I cannot stress enough the importance of little and often. Research has demonstrated that this approach is best, especially in the early stages of learning. You are far more likely to retain vocabulary that way. A marathon session of a couple of hours before class is far from ideal. Ten minutes three times a day is far more constructive.

- **Read regularly, even if it is just for a few minutes each day.** *Lingo Newydd,* a bimonthly magazine providing vocabulary lists alongside articles, is a good place to start. There will be articles to everyone's taste. Topics include fashion, sport, celebrities, nature, crafts and politics.

- **Work through a series of Welsh reading books as your knowledge grows,** starting with *Camu Ymlaen – Lefel 1 Mynediad* (Stepping Forward – Level 1 Entrance) edited by Meleri Wyn James. Even if you are an intermediate learner, it is good to start with a *Mynediad* reading book and use it as revision.

- **Move on to short novels for learners,** such as *Budapest* by

Elin Meek, and the novels of Bob Eynon, Bethan Gwanas and Pat Clayton. There are fiction and non-fiction books for learners, from chick lit to simplified poetry. Bethan Gwanas will sometimes include dialect, but this is always made clear in the vocabulary section at the end of the book. Browse in your local Welsh bookshop or go to the Gwales website for a selection. Further useful books, at a variety of levels, are listed in Appendix I.

- **Novels as audio books for learners are one of the best ways to begin reading in a second language.** Listening to the recording as you read along helps pronunciation, too. There are not many available in Welsh for learners, although some of Bob Eynon's books are still available with a cassette tape. For advanced learners, many of the classic Welsh writers' novels such as Kate Roberts, T. Rowland Hughes and Caradog Pritchard, are available on CD. You can find these on the Gwales website.

- **DVDs and television programmes** on the Welsh-language channel S4C and podcasts for learners from Radio Cymru (the Welsh-language radio channel) are more readily available and help build vocabulary. Use these as a learning resource with or without subtitles depending on your level. S4C has a useful website for learners at all levels. See Appendix II for links.

- **Gwales lists over two hundred Welsh-language e-books** but there is not a great deal available for learners as yet. Colin Jones' short novel *Coed y Brenin*, published by Cadw Sŵn, is available on Amazon Kindle. The e-book series, *Stori Sydyn*, could be useful for intermediate and advanced learners.

- **You may find the encouragement of other learners a help when reading.** Many Welsh-learning centres hold *clybiau darllen* (reading clubs) suitable for learners at various stages in their learning.

- **Are you on a budget and don't want to spend much on books or DVDs?** You could find these at your local library, if you live in Wales. If they are not available at your branch, ask the librarian to order them.

- **Beibl.net** – an online simplified version of the Welsh Bible for learners – is a free resource which will help extend vocabulary. A parallel hard copy of the text of Luke's Gospel in the Beibl.net version with the *Good News Bible* is particularly useful. Beibl.net became available in hard copy in 2015.

- *Wicipedia* (Welsh Wikipedia) provides useful reading material for the more advanced learner, see *cy.wikipedia.org/*. If you have been following S4C series, such as *Y Gwyll*, you may find a summary on the site to help reinforce vocabulary.

Keep a balance, though. Don't spend so much time on reading that you lose out at speaking. You could end up having what Gabriel Wyner describes as 'broken words'. In other words, words you have learned through reading and do not know how to pronounce. When you read a word, check out how to say it from the pronunciation rules. Then say the word aloud and check it with a Welsh speaker.

Most of the materials for learners include vocabulary lists. Even so, learners need at least one dictionary, such as *The Welsh Learner's Dictionary* by Heini Gruffudd or access to an electronic option such as *cysgair*, *geiriadur.net* or http://www.gutenberg.org/browse/languages/cy

Now don't be alarmed when I tell you that using a Welsh dictionary is not as straightforward as you would expect. You will soon get used to the difference.

The Welsh alphabet regards certain combinations of letters (linguists call them digraphs) as a single letter for the purposes of alphabetical listing. For example, all words beginning CH are alphabetised separately after C. This occurs even within words, so don't be too quick to say, as many of my students have over the years, 'It definitely wasn't in the dictionary.' The combinations to look out for are: ch, dd, ff, ng, ll, ph, rh, th.

'*Nghwm* starts with a C' is the title of Gaston Dorren's chapter on Welsh in his book, *Lingo*. Yes. We have to face the fact that Welsh, just like its Celtic cousins, sometimes changes consonants at the beginning of words. Now this could make life tricky for the new reader of Welsh. Books specifically geared to learners will usually give the original word, not the mutated version, in the vocabulary section. By the time learners are reading authentic material, they should know enough about mutations to cope.

All grammar books will explain the mutations and there is an invaluable laminated table, *Y Treigladur / The Mutation Map*, available for £2.99 from the Gwales website for those learners keen to check out the system.

The more you read, the more vocabulary you will acquire and, as you learn more language patterns, you can move on to more interesting, challenging books.

## Task

Before moving on to the next chapter, choose around six of the ten words or phrases in the Morris and Meara list that are the most useful for you and learn them until they are a part of you. If you have been learning for a while, check you know the plurals for all the words. Then try to use the words in phrases or sentences as soon as possible. Buy the book *Welsh Words: Core vocabulary with phrases*, making sure you choose the right version for your area, and learn and use the vocabulary recommended. Subscribe to the learners' magazine, *Lingo Newydd*, and read at least a paragraph every day. It is possible to buy the magazine in Welsh-language bookshops and in the larger branches of WH Smith.

### Want to find out more?

Steve Morris and Paul Meara, *Welsh Words: Core vocabulary with phrases* (Y Lolfa, 2014), available in north and south Walian versions.

Meleri Wyn James (ed.), *Ling di Long* (Y Lolfa, 2013) – a reading book for *Mynediad* / Entrance level.

Meleri Wyn James (ed.), *Mynd Amdani* (Y Lolfa, 2012) – a reading book for *Sylfaen* / Foundation level.

Meleri Wyn James (ed.), *Ar Garlam*, (Y Lolfa, 2012) – a reading book for *Canolradd* / Intermediate level.

*Beibl.net Efengyl Luc* (colloquial Welsh Gospel of Luke, with parallel *Good News Bible* English, Bible Society, Swindon, 2014).

*Beibl.net*, Cymdeithas y Beibl (2015).

Gaston Dorren, *Lingo* (Profile Books, 2014).

Heini Gruffudd, *The Welsh Learner's Dictionary* (Y Lolfa, 2009). Also available in a mini version.

Michael Grunberg, *Linkword Welsh* (Gwasg Gomer, 2000).

Guto Rees, *Treigladur / Mutation Map* (Ulpan, 2010).

Benny Lewis' blog: http://www.fluentin3months.com/

Tim Ferriss' blog: http://www.fourhourworkweek.com/blog/2009/01/20/learning-language/

http://www.thediceplace.com/

www.beibl.net

http://www.golwg360.com/cylchgronau-cwmni-golwg (to subscribe to *Lingo Newydd*)

Gwales.com

## Chapter 4

# Speed, slang, dialect and idioms – how to cope

### Speed

In Welsh, just as in other languages, issues such as speed of speech, use of slang, dialect and idioms are closely intertwined – it's just how real people talk! This is not a problem restricted to Wales – most fluent speakers are guilty of speaking too fast for learners. We may start off carefully but soon get carried away. It's easy to forget to speak at a steady pace, so that words and phrases no longer sound like those learners have discovered in class.

There is much discussion among teachers of English as a second language on the merits of slowing down speech for learners when teaching a group. Some tutors believe they should speak as they normally would in order to give learners exposure to the world outside the classroom. This means students won't be too shocked when they try to communicate in the real world. Some, for instance, Jon Lewis, who teaches English in France, go as far as recommending teaching colloquial forms such as *I wanna go* instead of *I want to go*. He argues that most learners want to speak; fewer are interested in writing.

I feel uneasy about this approach. While I sympathise with Jon Lewis in that he wants to get students communicating as quickly as possible outside class, I think he is putting the cart before the horse. Students need to learn standard language before the elisions and colloquialisms that lend themselves to speedy speech.

I believe students, in particular beginners, benefit from slowed down speech articulated precisely in class, especially if they are aiming for fluency. They can learn expressions such as *sa i'n gwybod* '*to* (I do not know yet) after the more formal form, *Dydw i ddim yn gwybod eto* has been learned and become a part of them. They will pick up colloquial forms as they mix with Welsh speakers.

A better solution to the speed issue would be for tutors to advise learners not to be afraid to ask Welsh speakers to slow down. Learners should ensure that the expressions (noted in Chapter 1) to use when people speak too quickly are second nature to them. I spoke to Meinir when conducting a vox pop at the National Eisteddfod (a Welsh-language cultural festival). As a first-language Welsh speaker, Meinir views Welsh-speakers' speed of speech as a great hindrance for learners. An experienced primary school teacher, she realises the importance of speaking at a steady pace. '*Rhaid siarad yn bwyllog'* (We need to speak at steady pace) is Meinir's advice to Welsh speakers.

Over time, of course, learners will be able to keep up with normal speed of speech as their vocabulary, knowledge of language patterns and confidence grows. It can be a shock when learners move from the classroom, where the tutor speaks slowly and clearly, to mix with native speakers who often have no idea how hard it is to hear what is being said in another language. The issue can, in part, be one of vocabulary and even formality as, even in classes that focus on communication, learners are not usually presented with very informal speech.

As stressed earlier, so many problems *dysgwyr* encounter are not restricted to learning Welsh. Anchee Min, a Chinese girl learning English in the US, writes in *The Cooked Seed*:

> I noticed that Kate and others never said, 'How do you do?' Instead they greeted each other with 'What's up dude?' I told Kate that I could not find 'What's up dude?' in my dictionary, or in *English 900 Sentences.* She laughed. 'It's a silly expression. A fun way of saying the same thing.' From then on I changed my greeting from 'How do you do?' to 'What's up dude?'

Now this was fine for Anchee when she was with her peers, but greeting an interviewer with 'What's up dude?' is unlikely to secure a job offer.

Listening to day-to-day conversations as much as possible will help. Listen to an English tutor in Japan, Julian, giving advice to English learners on YouTube: www.youtube.com/watch?v=flZ9K2wyXYk

Elision, the omission of sounds and syllables in speech, occurs in Welsh as in other languages and is part and parcel of talking quickly. This can be problematic for learners.

Edward Enfield (yes, Harry's father!) was frustrated when trying to make himself understood in the Greek he had picked up from Linguaphone. He found the Greeks frequently used elisions, saying the equivalent of *Give us another* in English as: *Gisser nuvver*. Most native speakers of any language run words together so that they no longer sound like those in class. Examples in English would be *I dunno* for 'I don't know' and *camra* for 'camera'.

Speed, therefore, is bound up with vocabulary and formality issues. The answer, as always, is practice, as the more exposure learners have to a variety of styles the better.

## Dialect and Slang

We now enter an area linked with speed that could be quite sensitive for some Welsh speakers. Some years ago one of my students told me of an angry exchange at one of the Cardiff libraries between two borrowers. One borrower, a north Walian had said that the word *cwympo* is slang. Now *cwympo* is a perfectly acceptable Welsh word for 'to fall', found in the dictionary and used regularly in south Wales. The north-Walian borrower used *syrthio,* the word he was familiar with which, as it happens, was also used in William Morgan's 1588 translation of the Bible.

There has been a tendency for some Welsh speakers to view the words chosen by William Morgan for his Bible translation as the only acceptable words for an object, concept or verb. This is not the case. If it were not for the William Morgan's translation and the subsequent standardising of the language, Welsh could well have divided into several dialects. In an era before media coverage and travel opportunities, we could have ended up with the situation where Welsh speakers in, for instance, Pembrokeshire could not understand Welsh speakers in Anglesey. This does not mean, however, that words not chosen by William Morgan are necessarily inferior or should be classed as slang. There are sometimes two words for exactly the same thing, e.g. *llwynog* and *cadno* for fox; one is not necessarily superior to the other but may be used more in certain regions of Wales.

In north Wales the word *budr* is used for dirty, but *brwnt* is used in the south. In the novel *William Jones* by T. Rowland Hughes, William, when arriving from the north, is surprised to hear men in the south refer to his brother-in-law as *bachgen budr*. In the south *budr* meant 'a bit of a character' and had nothing to do with being dirty.

While the chief dividing line is between north and south Wales, there are many regional differences in Wales, not merely in vocabulary but also in sounds and sentence structure. In Gwenhwyseg, the dialect of the Glamorganshire valleys and Gwent, for instance, the consonants 'g' and 'd' become 'c' and 't' so the word *cadair* (chair) is pronounced *'catar'* and *digon* (enough) is pronounced *'dicon'*.

In my experience as a tutor, these are the words and phrases that often trip up *dysgwyr*, even those who are quite experienced. They don't expect them and usually cannot find them in a dictionary. When I was a child in the south Wales valleys, I often heard people saying, *'Rwy'n mynd tsha thre nawr.'* I knew this meant I am going home now, but it was some years before I realised that this expression came from *'Rwy'n mynd tua adre nawr.'* It was common in south Wales to use *tsha thre* for going homewards. One of the earlier meanings of *tre* or *tref* was home, thus *tsha thre* comes from *tua thref* – towards home, homeward. These dialect expressions are still used in south Wales, especially in Glamorgan, but now *tsha thre* is sometimes used for 'at home' as well as 'homeward'.

There are also forms that can be regarded as slang expressions, often English words that have been Welshified in some way – words such as *joio, bishi* and *saff* (to enjoy, busy and safe). In colloquial Welsh it is quite common to take English words and add an 'o' or an 'io' to give them a Welsh flavour – for instance *practiso, crashio, dreifio, iwsio.*

Exposure and immersion are the answer, of course. If learners go out into their local community and mix with locals as much as possible as early as possible in their learning process, they will pick up expressions that are not in the dictionary. As time goes by they will learn when to use colloquialisms and regionalisms and when to use more formal language, in the work-place for example.

Even in our first language, we are not always familiar with regional expressions. For instance, I was not familiar with the English dialect word 'nesh' (unusually susceptible to cold weather) until I was in my forties, but it is a word familiar to most in the north of England.

Few *dysgwyr* will master Welsh and all the dialect and slang expressions, but over time they will learn enough to hold their own in a chat with the locals in their area.

Language learners tend to get daunted very easily if they do not know an expression. It is always best to think of language learning as an on-going journey. There's always going to be more to learn just as there is always more to learn about any topic in geography or history, for example. If mastering a language is viewed as an exciting journey, where new words and expressions interest and intrigue, the journey is no longer onerous but pleasurable.

There are several books and sections of books that are useful for learning about Welsh dialects, such as the following, but the best way is for the learner to integrate with the locals and imbibe naturally.

Beth Thomas and Peter Wynn Thomas, *Cymraeg, Cymrâg, Cymrêg... Cyflwyno'r Tafodieithoedd* (Gwasg Taf, 1989: out of print but available in libraries).

Alan R. Thomas, *Welsh Dialect Survey* (University of Wales Press, 2000).

Ceri Jones, *Dweud eich Dweud – A guide to Colloquial and*

*Idiomatic Welsh* (Gomer Press, 2013) – a very useful book for learners who want to know about various levels of formality in Welsh.

Some key regional differences for vocabulary used in north and south Wales are listed in Appendix III.

Welsh speakers need to be sensitive to learners' needs and ready to explain the meaning of any regional expressions they use.

## Idioms

Idioms are phrases that cannot be understood from the dictionary definition of each word taken separately. Examples of English idioms would be, 'to let the cat out of the bag' or 'to kick the bucket'. Most speech is littered with idioms, although we are usually unaware of this in our first language. Idioms enrich language but it will be a gradual process for learners coming to grips with a second language to imbibe them. Sometimes, a learner will be struggling to figure out how the idiom fits into the context of a conversation as they are taking the words literally. It is easy to cause confusion. Someone from overseas with excellent English thought my husband was keeping kittens in his office as I said he was having kittens there, meaning he was worried about something. The initial confusion and then the amusement when all is made clear actually helps learners to recall idioms.

In my experience as a tutor I have found that learners are very interested in idioms and enjoy finding out how they came into being. *Dim gobaith caneri* (not a canary's hope), the equivalent of saying in English 'Not a snowball's hope in hell,' is quite a favourite. The idiom refers to the old practice of taking canaries into mines as an early-warning system to test for the presence of toxic gases. While it takes time to acquire a wide range of idioms, there are many excellent books to help, in particular those by Cennard Davies.

In all of the areas we have been discussing in this chapter, learners may sometimes receive mixed messages from Welsh speakers. There will be a variety of views on which words and expressions are appropriate. Learners must choose their own path, just as in their first language.

Most fluent speakers are able to speak without using either regionalisms or idioms and should try to do so when speaking to learners at beginner level. When they use them with more advanced learners, they should be able to explain the meaning.

## Task

Buy or borrow one of the books below or explore the recommended internet sites below. Choose three idioms you think you will use in the future and learn them. Then learn an idiom a week. Collect all your idioms in your notebook.

**Good sources for idioms:**

Alun Cownie, *A Dictionary of Welsh and English Idiomatic Phrases: Welsh-English/English-Welsh* (Gwasg Prifysgol Cymru, 2012).

Leonard Hayles, *Welsh Phrases for Learners* (Y Lolfa, 2011).

Cennard Davies, *Cryno-ddysg y Cymry: Diarhebion ac Idiomau i Ddysgwyr* (Gwasg Prifysgol Cymru, 2002).

http://www.cardiff.ac.uk/languagezone/welsh/archivedarticles/welsh-sayings.html

http://www.madog.org/dysgwyr/gramadeg/gramadeg3.html

http://ssiw.pbworks.com/w/page/39929721/Welsh%20Idioms

**Other reading:**

Anchin Min, *The Cooked Seed* (Bloomsbury, 2014).

Edward Enfield, *Greece on my Wheels* (Summersdale, 2011).

# Chapter 5

# Practise, Practise, Practise

'My secret is practice. I always believed that if you want to achieve anything you have to work, work and then work some more.'

David Beckham, retired England footballer

'When I was a kid growing up I just played the flute all the time; it was like a bug, you know, like kids have their video games now, well I had a similar approach to the flute.'

James Galway, award-winning flautist

'The three great essentials to achieve anything worthwhile are: hard work, stick-to-itiveness and common sense.'

Thomas A. Edison, inventor

Glynne Jones, the charismatic musical director of Pendyrus choir for over thirty-eight years, was my music teacher when I was a child. Glynne expected his students to practise and there was no fooling him. If the piano pieces had not been practised and did not reach his expectation – which generally meant practising for at least half an hour a day – he would shout, 'Put it away. Put it away. Come back next week. Come back next week.' He would sometimes throw children's music books from the front door of his Dowlais home into the middle of the road, in exasperation that no practice had taken place since their last lesson.

Students who coped with Glynne's drama (and there weren't many!) did well. I liked music but had no great ear for it or sense of rhythm. Nonetheless I did well, even winning first prize in the school Eisteddfod one year and performing in the annual school concert. Several children with natural musical talent should have done much better than I but did not put in the practice time. It was all down to knowing that I had to either practise regularly or give up music, as Glynne would not continue teaching anyone who was lax in their attitude. There was no other music teacher within walking distance of my house, so I practised the same pieces over and over again until they were up to Glynne's standard, driving my telly-addict brother crazy.

Why am I telling you all this? Well, learning a language requires practice just as much as, if not more than, those music pieces I slaved over night after night. Experts Heini Gruffudd and Steve Morris of Swansea University estimate that 1,500 hours of exposure to Welsh are required for students to approach fluency. And of course any practice has to be in the 'real world' to gain confidence and 'street cred'.

Classes, the tutor and the student group are just the springboard, like my lessons with Glynne. Reading over the material learned in class, listening to it on CDs or podcasts, and then going out and using what you know in the real world are essential if speaking is the learner's aim.

The journalist Matthew Syed, who was the England number one table tennis player for many years, argues in his book *Bounce* that when we think of success we often cling to myths about innate ability and the true nature of talent. Matthew believes that it is practice, not talent, that actually matters. He draws on research studies and examples of high achievers from the worlds of sport and music to illustrate his point. One of the aims of his book is to demonstrate that we can all accomplish many things that seem far beyond our current capabilities with work and practice.

Matthew refers to Jack Nicklaus, arguably the most successful golfer of all time who made the same point: 'Nobody, but nobody, has ever become really proficient at golf without practice, without doing a lot of thinking and then hitting a lot of shots. It isn't so much a lack of talent; it's a lack of being able to repeat good shots consistently that frustrates most players. And the only answer to that is practice.'

Matthew asks, 'Where is the evidence for the pessimism emanating from those who make comments such as "I am not a natural linguist" or "I don't have the brain for numbers" or "I lack the coordination for sport"?' He believes it is often based upon nothing more than a few weeks or months of half-hearted effort.

I couldn't agree more. I began teaching languages in 1982 and over the years I've seen many students give up. Often they've said, 'I am thick,' or 'I'm hopeless at languages,' or 'I was useless at languages in school,' or 'I'll never be as good as so and so'. Like Matthew, I have noticed that the main reason they give up is lack of work and practice time. They nearly always expect it all to happen as if by magic. By turning up each week at class they thought they would be able to become fluent speakers. Wrong!

I have also noticed that some students, who carry on learning and have no intention of giving up, are constantly bemoaning how slow they are. Almost without exception, such students are not slow learners but expect too much progress too quickly. Olga now fluent in Hebrew following attendance at an intensive ULPAN course in Israel and with help from a mentor, stresses that learners should not have high expectations. Learners need time, patience and persistence. Even after nine years in Israel she is continuing to learn and bemoans the simplicity of her Hebrew in comparison to her

Olga from Russia – having a mentor helped her use Hebrew in the community.
Photo: Olga Smoldyreva

English. She knows enough about language learning to realise that, if she persists, she will improve and get to the stage of being able to discuss more complex topics in Hebrew.

According to Sir Chris Hoy, six-time Olympic champion, 'No one is born a champion, champions are made – through endless hard work and determination.' I can see the degree of fluency Olga aspires to in Hebrew, and which many Welsh learners desire as being close to championship level.

This will mean work and practice and will usually necessitate giving up other activities and commitments. If you really want to do something – anything – you will find the time. Give up a hobby, cut corners on housework and gardening, delegate tasks to the family or pay someone to help with these tasks, watch less television, read fewer novels, and you will find time. There may be some friends or relatives who will misunderstand your motives for spending less time over a latte with them. Some, on the other hand, may enjoy talking to you about learning Welsh and other languages and you may even inspire them to start learning.

You may not want such a high level of fluency of course, but be glad to simply get by in Welsh. We'll talk about degrees of fluency later, but remember that if you do want to be fluent enough to discuss even complex topics in Welsh, you will need to put in time and practice and be determined to persevere.

There is a tendency to think only talented people are able to learn Welsh, or any other language for that matter. Yes, many talented people are fluent in Welsh, but chat to these people and you will find that they, too, put in a great deal of time and effort on the long road to fluency, just as thousands of 'ordinary people' have.

Ideally, outside class, learners should spend some time studying and some time speaking in the community. Many are happy to study and do the homework for class but fail to practise their skills in the real world. One of the reasons for this in areas where there are few Welsh speakers is the lack of opportunity, especially if the learner has no family members or significant others who speak Welsh and their social circle is made up of English speakers. Again, determination is needed. Madison Tazu, Learner of the Year in 2008, moved to Brighton from Cardiff. She advertised in the local paper and found someone willing to practise Welsh with her. Where there's a will, there's a way.

Try not to let the opportunity for practising with Welsh speakers put you in the 'us and them' mentality. This is another issue not unique to Wales. In the USA English-language students sometimes struggle to find practice opportunities. Anchee Min from mainland China found that when she made friends she was able to extend her language skills, but it is difficult in the Western world to practise in the community when everyone is so busy.

Zongren Liu wrote of his experiences when trying to practise English in the USA in *Two Years in the Melting Pot*. At first he resorted to watching the television, even advertisements, to help him get to grips with day-to-day speech, as he found it difficult to engage English speakers in casual conversation. Though he was a lodger with an American family, he had little opportunity to converse as family members did not eat together but took trays to their rooms where they watched television or spent time on the computer. Only when a young couple befriended him did he really benefit from regular practice.

Another key issue for promoting success in any field is being in the right place at the right time. Matthew Syed points to the excellent table tennis teacher he had in school and the opportunity to practise 24/7 as his parents bought a table tennis table when he was young. For the Welsh learner, if there is a relative, neighbour or friend who is a Welsh speaker, this is an advantage that needs to be tapped into as soon as possible in the learning process. Having a mentor nearby is an invaluable resource.

Evolve a strategy with the Welsh speaker. Do not weary them; if you are a beginner, just five minutes twice a week practising what you've learned in class will help you. Build up to longer sessions as time goes by. Just reading aloud for a few minutes and having your pronunciation corrected is useful. If it is difficult to find a time in a busy schedule, try to set a regular time. If your mentor is a big *Pobol y Cwm* or *Archers* fan, plan to speak twice a week as soon as the programmes finish.

With your children do what Eben Muse did. Learn alongside them, refuse to speak English to them from the beginning and learn their nursery songs. Lisa Jones has written a useful book, *Welsh for Parents*, with three accompanying CDs that will help you learn Welsh with your children.

If you are quite advanced in your learning you may run out of ideas for conversation. Fluent-Forever.com/conversation-questions and ConversationStarter.com provide a handy list of conversation topics for language learners. There should be some topics to suit everyone.

Speak Welsh at home as you are walking around, e.g. *Dw i'n mynd lan lloft nawr* (I am going upstairs now). Talk to your pets in Welsh, e.g. *Ishte, Sbonc* (Sit down, Sbonc) and tell your pet about your day, e.g. *Enillodd Abertawe eto heddiw* (Swansea won again today). Read aloud as often as you can. The more exposure to the language, the more confident you will become.

Lisa Jones

The internet means that there has never been a better time to practise a language. If you really cannot find contacts for practice anywhere, there is always Skype.

Make the best use of the time you have. When Gabriel Wyner started learning French he cheated in the initial assessment because he used Google Translate and other forbidden tools. So he was placed in a high level group. Panic-stricken, he evolved a strategy. He looked at the time he had available until the course began – one hour a day for six days on the subway and one whole day. He made the very best use of this time and was able to reach beyond the level required for his group by the time his course started. According to Gabriel: 'The real challenge lies in finding a path that conforms to the demands of a busy life.'

## Tasks

1. Take a look at your commitments. How much time are you willing and able to assign to learning Welsh? Make a realistic plan of the time you can allocate each day. Don't worry if at this time it's a small allocation – even ten to fifteen minutes every lunch break will pay off over time.

2. Who will be your mentor? Think carefully about this. Then contact the person today. Delaying will give you cold feet. Again, if all you can allocate is five minutes over the phone each week, that will produce results over time.

**Other reading:**

Matthew Syed, *Bounce: The myth of talent and the power of practice* (Fourth Estate, 2011).

Zongren Liu, *Two Years in the Melting Pot* (China Press, 1988).

Heini Gruffudd and Steve Morris, *Canolfannau Cymraeg a Rhwydweithiau Cymdeithasol Oedolion sy'n Dysgu'r Gymraeg* (Academi Hywel Teifi, 2012).

Lisa Jones, *Welsh for Parents* (Y Lolfa, 2011).

Fluent-Forever.com/conversation-questions

ConversationStarter.com

## Chapter 6

# Time Pressure

### *Dal ati* / Stick at it

Despite my earlier comment, 'You will find the time', I am not unsympathetic to pressures of time. Family responsibilities, work, and tasks in house and garden all eat into time. The week goes by and all the good intentions to study and practise since the last class are easily swallowed up.

When I worked for the Open University as an assistant lecturer in Welsh, I took advantage of free courses for staff and enrolled on French and Spanish courses. Students learn at home and submit assignments but, three or four times a year, they meet the tutor and other students for a tutorial and, about eight times a year, meet for online tutorials. I always found that as the time for meeting my tutor and other students came closer, my work and practice time increased until the day before it became urgent. I found it difficult to work at the languages each day, apart from looking at my vocabulary notebook and listening to CDs, but as time went by I became better at it. The desire not to fall behind other students is very motivating, especially when you are a language tutor!

If lives are full we have to prioritise activities. In language learning, especially in the early stages, little and often is ideal. Bite-size sessions learning vocabulary, or phoning a friend for a few minutes' conversation practice do not eat too much into a busy lifestyle. I always kept a notebook in my bag or pocket so that there was something to revise at odd moments. I had CDs upstairs and downstairs so that I could hear French or Spanish as I was getting ready to go out or when I was doing housework. I had another CD in the car so that I was constantly exposing myself to language as I was going about my daily tasks. Most people have smartphones or tablets these days and these can also be used at odd moments while waiting for a medical appointment or at the hairdressers, for instance.

Sometimes life throws many difficult things at us all at once. Just when we think we have a good window for language learning and practice, a family crisis blows up or work pressures increase. At such times language learning is likely to go to the bottom of the list as we struggle to survive and keep on top of our regular tasks. These are the times when we are tempted to give up altogether but it is important not to give in to negative thoughts and just keep ticking over until the pressure lifts.

In these situations, organisation is the key. Keep some Welsh material with you at all times and just keep listening as much as you can to Welsh, either from CDs, Radio Cymru, S4C or online. Try to learn a word, a phrase or an idiom each day. Put these in your notebook and revise them in free odd moments, such as in the bus queue or waiting for your coffee. It is important to *dal ati* (stick at it) even if you just fit in a few minutes each day so that you don't lose what you have learned.

## Tasks

What Welsh material will you have with you at all times? As well as your notebook, decide on something you will listen to on your phone or other device. Decide now before you move on to the next chapter – download the app or buy / borrow a CD.

## Chapter 7

# Anxiety

'When you learn somebody's language you're saying that you're prepared to sound foolish in order to communicate with them.'

Eitan Shishkoff, Hebrew learner

Practising a language is a very public thing to do and often provokes anxiety even in the most level-headed of learners. Adult learners dread looking foolish. Those who cope well in their daily lives and progress well in a Welsh classroom may become anxious when speaking outside class. Indeed high achievers, competent in the workplace and at home may be extremely anxious. They are used to being on top of things and do not want to lose face. The fear factor then impairs their performance.

Experts increasingly stress the issue of anxiety in language learning, many believing that it plays a bigger role for learners in the community than it does in class. 'Willingness to communicate' is considered vital for second-language learners' successful development of oral skills.

Learners tell of their minds going blank when they have an opportunity to use Welsh and a feeling of panic out of all proportion to the situation they are in. Some learners are anxious in specific settings only, such as the workplace or with close family members.

When I taught in the workplace I came across learners in senior positions who became so anxious that they gave up learning very early in the process. Often they did not make as much progress as their junior colleagues and did not want to appear foolish. They often viewed themselves as poor language learners, whereas the usual reason for their poorer progress was lack of time for practice because of a heavy work schedule, which often extended into evenings and weekends, and their family responsibilities.

In focus group discussions, anxiety about talking in Welsh to family members, significant others and close friends is often mentioned. Learners feel uncomfortable as 'they knew them first in English'.

Life crises, such as the hospitalisation of a close relative, may cause otherwise confident learners to falter. I remember one self-assured learner who lost confidence using Welsh when his child was admitted to hospital and over quite a long period there was uncertainty about the prognosis.

Usually, though, there is no such trigger for the anxiety a learner feels when using Welsh. One of the main reasons for the problem is the concern about accuracy. This was my problem before I became a fluent Welsh speaker. I had a 'head' knowledge of Welsh but was worrying too much about being accurate instead of getting on with speaking. I thought I had to get all my mutations and genders correct before communicating. How wrong! I have told my story elsewhere in

the book, *Think Without Limits: You CAN speak Welsh*, but suffice to say here that, when I took the plunge and started using what I knew without worrying unduly about accuracy, precision followed.

Communication is what is needed first and foremost. Maybe we don't remember if 'chair' is masculine or feminine in Welsh. This does not stop people realising we are talking about the chair.

Think without Limits – you CAN speak Welsh.

We need to get speaking, practising and using what we know regularly. Accuracy will develop over time. Don't expect too much too quickly. Think in terms of years rather than weeks and months. You have become involved in a lifetime's project. Complete fluency in a second language – that is the ability to discuss any topic under the sun – takes years of practice. However, you can enjoy using words and phrases from the start. Remember, having people to speak back to you is one of your main aims. I get a real buzz when native speakers respond to my faltering Spanish and French. This spurs me on to learn more and use the language I have.

Communication is often a struggle for me in French despite the high marks I gained on my Open University module. Using French is fine on paper, and even for an oral examination when all the topics are prepared, but when I start talking in the real world, that's different. We recently stayed in a self-catering complex in Corsica. Our hosts, Christophe and Marie-Laure and family, lived on the complex. I was very pleased with myself on the first day when I reported to Christophe's daughter in French that the light bulb had failed in our bathroom and we needed a replacement. No English passed our lips so I was left wondering if she had understood. Christophe appeared a few hours later with the appropriate substitute so I knew I'd got it right. Flushed with success, I spoke French to quite a few people on the trip and survived. I am not particularly anxious using French abroad but, strangely, I am quite nervous about using it with French speakers in the UK. It is all to do with not wanting to look foolish and sounding ridiculous.

I referred to Wynne Evans earlier and his clear communication skills in Welsh despite some grammar inaccuracies. Another such clear communicator is Richard Harrington, the heart-throb of the dark mystery series, *Y Gwyll*. Now by his own admission Richard was a bit of a *bachgen drwg* (naughty boy) in school and did not invest enough time in study. That's probably why, when interviewed, he sometimes does not mutate or get the gender right.

These errors, though, in no way detract from the interesting things he has to say about his origins in Merthyr Tydfil and his life in London and Cardiff. Fluent communication is far, far more important than remembering whether the word *awr* is feminine and should be preceded by *dwy, tair* and *pedair* rather than *dau, tri*, and *pedwar.*

Richard's parents did not speak Welsh but sent Richard to a Welsh-medium school and his Welsh flows like one who has been brought up in a Welsh-speaking home.

Zoe Pettinger, finalist in the Learner of the Year competition in 2009, gives the following advice to learners:

> Don't worry if you make mistakes. The most important thing is to speak the language instead of worrying about the accuracy of the language. How many people in England speak the Queen's English? We all speak with different dialects and use sentences which are not totally grammatically perfect. If you are corrected, remember the correction and you will be able to develop your linguistic skills. It is a good way to learn.

Learners tend to be purists in their use of Welsh, much more so than many Welsh speakers who often use English words – or Welshified words such as *practiso*, in everyday speech, a custom common among bilinguals the world over. On Radio Cymru, Welsh speakers often use English words for numbers, so much so that a friend in Ludlow once asked if the Welsh had their own words for numbers.

Basil Davies, one of the early pioneers of teaching Welsh to adults, used to tell students, 'If you are waiting for the day when you will speak perfectly before you start having a conversation, you are waiting for a day that will never arrive.'

Rachel Jones, originally from London, is a case in point. When she began learning she decided she would not speak until she was absolutely accurate but came to realise that, if she persisted in this way, she would never speak at all.

Learners, then, need to be less anxious about accuracy; they need to relax and enjoy using Welsh. View every mistake as an opportunity to learn something new and concentrate on the message rather than the medium.

This is not always as easy as it sounds. Adult anxiety and lack of confidence when learning new languages is so prevalent that it has even been given a name: language shock. American researchers report that foreign-language classes are the most anxiety-provoking of all. Students learning Japanese made statements such as: 'It's only in Japanese class I feel so nervous'; 'I study a lot. But, my brain becomes blank when I have to say something in Japanese'; and 'I've never been so nervous in other classes.'

Various reasons have been put forward to explain these feelings. People who are competent in their native language feel anxious about producing childlike statements in the second language. This was certainly the case in the interviews and focus group discussions for my own research – where some students reported feeling frustrated as well as anxious communicating in Welsh. They bemoaned the fact that their speech in Welsh was childlike and that they could not find the words they needed to express an idea.

Psychoanalysts, even as far back as the 1930s, believed that adults feared using a second language because they didn't want to appear comic. One such – a Professor Stengal – likened an adult learning a second language to a person wearing fancy clothes. The adult learner may want to wear his fancy clothes but is inhibited by fear of ridicule and criticism. The child, on the other hand, views language as a form of play and enjoys wearing fancy clothes. The more adults have preserved these 'infantile characteristics', the more easily they will learn.

The author C. S. Lewis held that the most mature among us are those who have lost the fear of seeming childish. He wrote, 'When I became a man I put away childish things, including the fear of childishness and the desire to be very grown up.' It is certainly my experience as a tutor that the students who are willing to take risks and experiment with language, even to the extent of making themselves look foolish, are often the more successful language learners in the long term.

So how can Welsh learners overcome anxiety? Here are some suggestions that will help.

## Top Tips for Anxious Learners

- **Start practising from day one**. *Sut mae! ... dw i. Pwy dych chi?* (Hi, I'm ... What is your name?) *Mae hi'n braf heddi* (It's fine today). Just saying these short sentences aloud outside class will build confidence.

- **Find a person (a mentor) for practising.** Evolve a strategy. Arrange when you will speak and build up gradually starting with two-minute sessions, even if it's only five or ten minutes a week on the phone or on Skype in the early stages of learning. This will reinforce what you learn in class and boost your confidence.

- **Fix up Welsh-only sessions, starting with bite-size sessions of three minutes** if you have family and close friends you see regularly who are fluent speakers.

- **Have phrases ready** (from Chapter 1) to use with Welsh speakers.

- **Try to find a group of learners who meet up regularly to practise in your area.**

- **Join a Welsh-medium activity** such as a choir, sports or board games. The local *Menter Iaith* (see Appendix IV) will supply you with a list.

- **Listen to as much Welsh as possible** on S4C, Radio Cymru, Podcasts, CDs. Even eavesdrop on fluent speakers in cafés, shops and the hairdressers. In fact, whenever you hear a Welsh conversation, listen in as discreetly as possible. Listening is a non-threatening way to build confidence. I do this often when travelling in Europe. This usually works, though sometimes I confess it can result in funny looks! Ideally, it is best to start speaking using short words and simple phrases from day one. However, if you are very anxious it is probably a good idea to just listen for a while initially.

- **Use the sub-titles on S4C** if you are in the early stages of learning but try to wean yourself off them as time goes by. Use the S4C website for learners, too.

- **Read a little Welsh each day.** This is another non-threatening way to build confidence. If possible, read aloud with a fluent speaker and ask them to correct any pronunciation errors. Even a few sentences will help. There are recommendations for learners of all levels in Chapter 3 and in more detail in Appendix I.

- **Say something aloud in Welsh each day.** If you live alone talk to yourself. Make some short recordings and ask fluent speakers to listen to them and correct errors. If you have a pet tell it about your day and your plans etc. Learn how to give the pet commands in Welsh.

- **Learn some vocabulary each day, even if it is just one word.** The wider your vocabulary the more confident you will feel in the real world. Problems with listening skills are often caused by limited vocabulary.

- **Speak simply if you are a beginner and do not try to translate from English or your mother tongue.** Use simple phrases from books such as *Live Welsh* by Heini Gruffudd.

- **Try to learn words in context** i.e. in short phrases or sentences.

- **If you are not attending a course** during the long summer gap, try to take up the summer challenge (*her yr haf*). Set yourself tasks to do before the September course begins. Your tutor will be able to suggest activities for you to do that will keep your Welsh alive, either on your own or with others.

- **Keep your eyes open for bilingual signs.** Note any new words or phrases that you see, especially those useful to you. Be careful though, sometimes there are mistakes to spot!

- **Keep a learning journal in English or your mother tongue.** This may help you understand when and why you become anxious or why you react in a certain way. I kept a learning journal some years ago when I was in Germany which I summarised in my book *Think Without Limits: You CAN speak Welsh* and found it useful.

- **Keep a Welsh diary.** Try to write at least one simple sentence a day, e.g. *Mae hi'n heulog heddiw* (It's sunny today). When you have learned the past tense, write a sentence each day about something you've done, e.g. *Es i i'r pwll nofio heno* (I went to the swimming pool tonight). Don't worry if you are repeating yourself and just saying, *Dw i'n mynd i'r swyddfa heddiw* (I am going to the office today). Keep writing something each day.

- **Laugh at mistakes** and see them as part of the learning process. Learners who take risks and make mistakes will make much faster progress than those striving to be perfect before they speak.

- **Have a go at speaking with someone!** Throw caution to the wind and try out your Welsh on a fluent speaker. There's everything to gain and nothing to lose apart from possibly sounding a little silly occasionally. Does that really matter? It will get easier the more you do it.

Nate Nicholson, author of *How to Become Fluent in any Language in a Few Months*, writes:

> The sooner you get over your fear and start doing it, the sooner you become fluent. There's no workaround. Quick results are all about conversational practice. One thing that helps me get over my fears and speak with native speakers is to never hesitate. Whenever I have an opportunity to practise my skills, I don't give myself time to think about it. I just do it, because the longer I wait, the scarier it will be.

Nate is right. Hesitating doesn't help. It's a bit like going into the swimming pool and waiting before getting your shoulders under in the hope it will get warmer and easier. It doesn't. It gets colder and harder. Nate continues:

> You have to instil in yourself the belief that it's OK to make a fool out of yourself. You have to swallow your pride when you're speaking another language. You're going to make mistakes, you're going to sound ridiculous and you're going to be misunderstood. All these things are necessary, as they help you learn from your mistakes and improve your skills.

So it's over to you. Go for it and have fun!

## Task

Speak to someone in Welsh today. Prepare what you want to say and then go for it. Do not think about it once you've prepared. If there is no one available, phone or Skype.

# Chapter 8

# Culture

'Tell me and I forget. Teach me and I remember.
Involve me and I learn.'
Benjamin Franklin

Learners won't have progressed far into gaining knowledge of the Welsh language before they realise there is more to learning a language than mere communication. Every language represents a unique culture. That is not to say that there is a single set of Welsh cultural norms which all mother-tongue Welsh speakers and learners should embrace. Cultural emphases vary across time and from one individual to the next.

Some learners and mother-tongue speakers have rigid views on what constitutes Welsh culture. One of my students was shocked, almost to the point of annoyance, because I was not interested in rugby and had not realised there was an international match taking place in Cardiff the following Saturday. I want Wales to win of course but, as far as I am concerned, the best part of the rugby match is the singing, and I cannot force myself to like rugby. In the same way, I cannot force others to enjoy male voice choirs, Welsh hymns, harp music and the novels of Islwyn Ffowc Elis.

There will be some aspect of Welshness that will appeal to each learner whether in the area of sport, religion, entertainment, traditional crafts, literature, old customs or history. Traditional Welsh culture for the majority of Welsh speakers was bound up with chapel life and eisteddfodau in the past. Nowadays, though this is still the case to a degree, new spheres of cultural interest are emerging, for instance dancing and pop music bands. Welsh is also making inroads into the world of business and commerce. If learners feel excluded from one sphere of culture, there will be many others to choose from.

By becoming involved in some aspect of Welsh culture that appeals to you, you are on the road to enhancing your linguistic skills. Culture is often bound up with socialising so this is a good chance to use what you've learned and enjoy yourself. The local *Menter Iaith* will give you details, as will tutors. For women, the local branch of *Merched y Wawr* (equivalent of the Women's Institute) provides the ideal opportunity to learn more about Wales and its culture while socialising with Welsh speakers. If you live in England you may be able to get to some Welsh groups, too. There are Welsh societies in London, Reading, Oxford, Birmingham, Liverpool, Manchester, Newcastle, Derby and Nottingham, and several other places. Jonathan Simcock has set up a Facebook page to support learners in England: https://www.facebook.com/groups/31395206651/

Holidays in west and north Wales with a Welsh-speaking family are also an excellent way of enhancing linguistic skills, imbibing local culture and having fun.

Gabriel Wyner stresses what should be obvious to all, 'We learn

Dysgwyr Derby.
Photo: Jonathan Simcock

better when we are having fun.' So it would be good for all learners to find some sphere of cultural interest they enjoy and become involved. Zoe Pettinger followed this path:

> Learning Welsh wasn't a chore for me at all. I had lots of fun while learning. I made lots of new friends. I discovered a new exciting world, filled with music, theatre, literature, games, social events and an incredible culture! Learn Welsh and stick with it and you too will experience an exciting new adventure.

Lists of useful contacts for learners to socialise and learn more of Welsh culture are in Appendix IV.

## Task

Look at the list in Appendix IV. What will suit you? Choose something. Perhaps another learner will go along with you to an event. Whatever you choose, stick at it. It may be hard initially, but perseverance will pay off.

If you cannot find something from the websites ring your local *Menter Iaith* office or e-mail them and ask for suggestions.

## Chapter 9

# Welsh speakers switching to English

'If you want to learn a language quickly, there's no other
way to do it than by speaking with natives as soon as possible.
It's scary, it's uncomfortable, but it's the most effective way to
improve your skills quickly!'

Nate Nicholson

I suppose I must be what is known as a *ieithgi* (a language dog), in other words someone who is very keen on languages, a linguist. I am fluent in English and Welsh – and Wenglish of course! – and when I'm in practice I'm quite good at communicating in German. But I also dabble in French and Spanish and, to a lesser degree, Greek, Italian and Russian. In fact I always try to use a few words of the local language wherever I go, though sometimes I am reduced to little more than a thank you as in Hebrew (*toda*), Arabic (*shukran*) and Norwegian (*takk*).

My efforts are greeted with varying degrees of delight, shock and amusement. I was pleased with myself in Zakynthos when I could ask for water without gas, *nero choris anthracico*. Every time I asked for this the waiter laughed, though he knew what I wanted. What was so funny? I never found out.

When I was out and about other Greeks seemed delighted with my efforts, one lady declaring, 'She speaks good Greek,' even though I knew little more than the fifty words I had learned on the plane from listening to Elisabeth Smith's *One-Day Greek* CD. Most people are thrilled that a visitor is having a go and are encouraging.

Now, I was not too bothered about the waiter laughing. I probably did not pronounce correctly or did not put the stress in the right place. Who knows? For me, dabbling in language is fun. I'm willing to have a go and do not take it too seriously.

It is different for many Welsh learners. Some have never learned another language or may have had bad experiences of learning French in school. When they go out into the community and take the plunge with a Welsh speaker, the last thing they want is someone laughing at them. The Welsh speaker usually means no harm and may just be feeling uncomfortable, particularly if they know the learner well. Learners, even those close to fluency, say it is particularly difficult to switch to speaking Welsh with family members and close friends.

Learners who can laugh if they have made a mistake that sounds funny to a fluent speaker are likely to progress more quickly than those who take it too much to heart. Over the years, several students, when asked what they did before class, have said, *Bwytais i'r gath* (I ate the cat) instead of *Bwydais i'r gath* (I fed the cat). Now if you can laugh at yourself for eating the cat you are halfway there.

What I find particularly difficult, though, is when native speakers turn to English when I am speaking in German, a language where I can communicate fluently on day-to-day matters. Some years ago I was at a railway station in Halberstadt, East Germany, and held a fairly lengthy conversation with the clerk behind the counter about places I could visit by train – length of the journey, times etc. This went well. Then I asked in German which platform I needed for my current journey. '*Fünf*,' she said. I thanked her and then she said, 'Five,' and held up her hand, pointing at five fingers. I had the pricked balloon feeling.

Later in Goslar, a lady asked where I was from during a full flow German conversation. When I said Wales she immediately turned to English. This was not quite so deflating, as I could see she just wanted to practise English – it was not a reflection on the standard of my German.

On a visit to Berlin I came out of the *Damentoiletten* in a highly excited state. I could not wait to tell my husband and two friends that a German lady had asked me, *'Woher in Deutschland kommen Sie?'* (Where in Germany do you come from?) after I had uttered a couple of sentences. I could not believe she actually thought I was German.

So these little things matter to us as second-language speakers. We are all sensitive to a greater or lesser degree about our language skills and we need a pat on the back from time to time.

The lady in the station was making doubly sure I got to the right platform. She was only being helpful, nothing for me to feel deflated about. But that is how we are as learners, we can feel discouraged very easily.

If Welsh speakers confirm arrangements in English, it is not necessarily a reflection on the learners' Welsh but just because it is something important. It is so easy for misunderstandings to arise when making arrangements, even in one's mother tongue. Whatever the standard of a learner's Welsh, it is advisable to confirm arrangements and appointments in English.

With the possible exception of some pre-school children, Welsh speakers are always fluent in English, so unlike the lady in Goslar they do not have the excuse they want to practise their English when they switch from Welsh.

So why do native Welsh speakers switch to English with learners? First, let us look at this globally. Problems communicating with the locals are not unique to Wales. When we visited Israel our tour guide, who had attended a five-month intensive Hebrew ULPAN course on a kibbutz, still had trouble persuading locals to speak to her in Hebrew. Olga, a Russian with excellent English, is something of a *ieithgi*. Yet many Israelis and Arabs insisted on using English to communicate with her. However, she persevered and found one person who practised Hebrew with her every week and built up her confidence. She now chats regularly in Hebrew in Israel.

Miquel Strubell de Trueta, a lecturer in the Department of

Languages and Cultures at the Open University of Catalonia, complains that fluent speakers turn to Spanish when learners are practising their classroom Catalan in the community.

In China, English speakers trying to practise Chinese struggle to find someone willing to chat in Chinese, so keen are the locals to improve their English.

We could go on with examples, but suffice to say that the problems of using a second language beyond the classroom are certainly not unique to Wales. In Patagonia, Welsh learners find that native speakers will often revert to Spanish, depriving them of much-needed practice. Welsh learners are less likely to take things personally when they understand that this phenomenon occurs elsewhere.

One significant reason Welsh learners, who have successfully completed courses in Wales, give for ceasing to use their classroom Welsh is the lack of opportunity to practise the language in the community. Many complain it is difficult to persuade first-language speakers to hold a conversation in Welsh. This complex issue is not one for apportioning blame to first-language speakers and/or learners.

Writing in *Taliesin*, Professor Bobi Jones, the first Welsh learner to become a professor of Welsh, stressed that integration of learners is the way forwards if the language is to gain ground. Bobi has expressed the view on many occasions that intervention from Welsh speakers is vital but it has to be *yn y galon* (in the heart) and *nid yn null y tân siafins* (not with transient enthusiasm). Do they really want to help learners? They must be persuaded to see language survival not just as an issue for campaigners but the responsibility of every Welsh speaker regardless of age, ability or language history.

Help for learners is as crucial to the future of the language as were the language campaigns in the 1960s, according to Bobi. In fact, he has predicted that the fortunes of the Welsh language could change if language protestors were also able to give one hour a week to provide learners with much-needed conversation practice.

> *Ond fe ŵyr hyd yn oed y protestwyr mae ewyllys barhaol y bobl yn unig i 'wneud' drostynt eu hun sydd yng nghanol Adennill yr Iaith. Dim arall. Ac y mae gweithredu effeithio yn golygu bod y Cymry Cymraeg rhugl mwyaf brwd yn estyn llaw cymdeithas – yn benderfynol, yn drefnus, ac yn barhaol i'r Dysgwyr. Nid yn null y tân siafins, ond yn sefydlog. Rhythm gwahanol sydd ei angen i'r dyfodol. Gyda'i gilydd y maent yn ffurfio'r Adennill.*

(Even the protestors know that only people's enduring will to take action themselves is central to language renewal. Nothing else will do. To effect this, the most enthusiastic fluent Welsh-speaking Welsh people must extend a sociable hand to learners – in a determined, orderly and enduring way. Not with transient enthusiasm, but consistently. A different rhythm is needed for the future. Together they can bring about renewal.)

As Bobi emphasises, practice is vital if learners are to metamorphise into fluent speakers. We must find a way to bring native speakers and learners together and help them understand one another's needs. Let's take a look now at why some native speakers are reluctant to use Welsh with learners. (In the next chapter some solutions will be suggested.)

It is widely known that language learners lack confidence when trying to use what they learn in class. It is not generally known that some native speakers of a lesser used language, such as Welsh, also lack confidence. As noted, some fluent Welsh speakers have never studied Welsh but only learned *ar yr aelwyd* (on the hearth) and often use English words such as *stasiwn* where the learners use *gorsaf* (station). When I was conducting a vox pop at the National Eisteddfod, one Welsh speaker who is close friends with an almost fluent learner said, 'I'm terrified of learners! They use big words.' Another lady said, 'I only speak Llanelli Welsh. They speak book Welsh.' Such attitudes are widespread.

When I have been trying to encourage Welsh speakers to come to chat with learners at a *Siop Siarad*, a group where learners practise the language they have learned in class, many have protested that their Welsh would not be of a good enough standard. It is easier to persuade fluent learners to come to a session. Helpers working at Menter Cwm Gwendraeth come across many who protest, *'Dydy fy Nghymraeg i ddim yn ddigon da i ddysgwyr.'* (My Welsh isn't good enough for learners.)

As noted, there is an attitude abroad that learners speak 'too posh'. This emerged from my research where Welsh speakers said that learners' Welsh was 'too accurate', 'so perfect', 'too correct', 'too good' and is borne out by recent research by S4C. Sioned Wyn Roberts, Content Commissioner for S4C said:

> *Mae un peth yn amlwg o'r ymchwil – mae llawer o siaradwyr Cymraeg yn poeni nad yw eu Cymraeg nhw'n ddigon da ac felly mae'n anodd magu hyder i siarad.*
>
> (One thing is obvious from the research – many Welsh speakers worry that their Welsh is not good enough and so it is difficult to gain confidence to speak.)

Many *Cymry Cymraeg*, bilingual since childhood, have no experience of learning a second language as an adult, so have no idea how difficult it is for learners. This could result in unrealistic expectations. Some learners have told me that after attending a two-hour a week course for a year, *Cymry Cymraeg* have said, 'Aren't you fluent yet?'

Welsh for adults tutors know it takes a long time to be fluent in any second language and are trained to know what it feels like to learn a new language. As part of their training, tutors are expected to participate in lessons in a language totally unknown to them, such as Gaelic, Catalan or Czech.

*Cymry Cymraeg* who have had little experience of Welsh

Diana Gruffydd-Williams, a fluent learner speaking in Welsh to learners about her book, *My People's Pilgrimage*, at Oriel Canfas, Cardiff.

learners are unsure of how much learners know. This, of course, will vary considerably from learner to learner. They may speak especially slowly to a fluent learner, explaining what they view as difficult words, or they may speak far too fast for a learner who has only been at it for a short time.

We have already touched on the importance of pronunciation. Retaining some accent is fine. We all know folk from overseas who speak English well but retain something of their accent whether it be French, Italian, Greek or German. However, if the pronunciation is so weak that we are straining to follow what the learner is saying, even though they have a good command of English, we don't want to know, do we?

It is the same with Welsh speakers struggling with learners whose pronunciation is hardly recognisable and whose stress and intonation are constantly wrong. I have taught learners who are often very capable and have a good 'head' knowledge of Welsh, but switch off when I correct pronunciation. Some 'book smart' learners are just not interested in learning that the stress is almost invariably on the last syllable but one in Welsh. They regard such details as a hindrance to them moving on. Although such learners are quite rare, should *Cymry Cymraeg* encounter them, they may well become wary of learners generally.

Sometimes *Cymry Cymraeg* are just too busy to speak to learners in Welsh in the work context, for instance where technical language is used and it is important that work tasks are completed efficiently with no misunderstandings.

Some *Cymry Cymraeg* may be impatient and may not want to know about learners. There are parochial people in all groups and the Welsh are no exception. Fortunately, my research has led me to the conclusion that such people are unusual in Wales and that most *Cymry Cymraeg* support learners and are thrilled that they are making the effort to learn, but do not always know how to help them.

Learners must see the 'switch issue' as part of a global problem for language learners and not take it personally. It does not necessarily mean their language skills are weak or that Welsh speakers do not want to include them in their social circle.

So, let us look at some solutions to the problems facing learners and *Cymry Cymraeg*.

## Chapter 10

# How to stop the switch

'Welsh speakers are too fussy by far! I believe that a
language is to be spoken regardless of minor mistakes,
communication is the whole point. Then later on maybe one
can look at the small details of putting the mutation in the
right place... etc! I always speak Welsh to learners regardless
of the hard work! I am so glad that they are trying.'

Sioned Glyn, first-language Welsh speaker

A few years ago I was delighted to contribute to the booklet
*Rhannwch eich Cymraeg* (Share your Welsh), a Welsh Government
initiative written by the staff of *Canolfan Cymraeg i Oedolion Caerdydd
a Bro Morgannwg* (The Cardiff and Vale Centre for Teaching Welsh
to Adults). The free booklet advises Welsh speakers on how to help
learners and provides guidance on speaking to learners at different
levels. Sample dialogues are included. As the message about the
importance of native speakers' contributions to learners' progress
spreads, things should improve. If learners are able to persuade
any Welsh speakers they know to read this booklet, their practice
opportunities should be more fruitful. Some tips for Welsh speakers
from the booklet are included in Appendix V.

The onus is on the learner, though, to persuade Welsh speakers to
help them by carrying on speaking in Welsh. Successful learners insist
on speaking Welsh even when Welsh speakers switch to English. Tim
Jilg from Ohio struggled with Welsh speakers who turned to English
but he persisted in always speaking Welsh to them, whatever their

Sioned Glyn, artist and first-language Welsh speaker.
Photo: Sioned Glyn

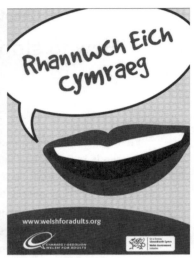

Rhannwch Eich Cymraeg.

reaction. He knew he needed the practice. Eventually they would respond in Welsh. Tim went on to become a fluent speaker and write his PhD in Welsh.

Eben Muse from Cape Cod, now a fluent Welsh speaker who works at Bangor University through the medium of Welsh, decided when his first child was born that he would only ever speak Welsh to his offspring.

If learners just have one person initially for practice opportunities, then confidence to use Welsh outside class will develop. Alison Layland, Learner of the Year in 1998, recommends this as does one of the early pioneering Welsh for adults tutors, Cennard Davies. When learning Hebrew, Olga found it invaluable to have one person, a mentor she visited each week to give her practice. It certainly boosted her confidence.

As confidence increases and knowledge grows, learners can build up to speaking to more people. If they have practised with a sympathetic person, then they are more likely to insist on speaking

Joella Price, Learner of the Year 2014.
Photo: Joella Price

Welsh if they find Welsh speakers switch to English when they are out and about.

Finding a mentor, formally or informally, through networking will help. If there is no one in your area, you could, as noted, practise on the phone or through Skype.

There are many societies where Welsh is spoken – choirs, churches, chapels and sports clubs. Attendance at *Merched y Wawr* sessions has helped many learners build confidence to use the Welsh they know. *Mentrau Iaith* arrange a wide variety of activities through the medium of Welsh from studying *cynghanedd* (strict-metre poetry) to *swmba* (zumba).

Joella Price, Learner of the Year in 2014, stresses the importance of belonging to a group. She attends *Clonc yn y Cwtsh* at the Chapter Arts Centre in Cardiff for three hours each week and knows this has helped her Welsh skills develop. Attending a local group regularly will improve speaking skills rapidly, vocabulary will be extended and confidence to continue speaking in Welsh when Welsh speakers switch will develop.

Parents with children have opportunities to chat with other parents, children and teachers before and after school and at a variety of functions. Attending *amser stori* (story time) in libraries and cafés with young children also offers some speaking practice. When mixing with other parents it is important to insist on speaking Welsh, only turning to English to ask about a word or expression that is unfamiliar or for important arrangements such as collecting children.

In the workplace, as indicated earlier, discussing work and business issues could result in misunderstandings and slow down progress. But there is no reason for not using Welsh socially. A few sentences in the lunch hour or a chance meeting in the corridor will help. Discuss how your children are getting on, or the match the previous weekend, or a film you've seen.

It would be good if more cafés, shops and pubs could advertise when Welsh speakers are available to speak to learners. Some do already but more are needed. Various badges for learners and Welsh speakers have been available over the years, though I must admit that on only three occasions has someone approached me and spoken Welsh as a result of my badge. This is an area that needs promotion and development. Eddy Hunt wrote to the *South Wales Echo*: 'Finding a Welsh-language service is a bit like looking for a needle in a haystack. The absence of obvious indicators such as badges (80 per cent of employers never offer one) doesn't help.' (See http://www.walesonline.co.uk/incoming/south-wales-echo-letters-thursday-8583627)

Hubs where learners and Welsh speakers are able to chat informally are starting to spring up in Wales. Hopefully these ventures will help to make relations between learners and Welsh speakers more relaxed. *Yr Hen Lyfrgell* in Cardiff has a café, a shop and function rooms where classes and other Welsh-medium activities and entertainment take place. To find out more go to: http://yrhenlyfrgell.cymru/. A similar centre in west Wales is *Atom* in Carmarthen and in the north-east *Camu* in Wrexham, which is more geared to promoting Welsh in the workplace. Check out whether there are similar centres where you live by ringing your local *Menter Iaith* office.

Even when all the guidance in this chapter is followed, if learners have not followed the advice in Chapter 2 about getting pronunciation right and picking up the rhythm of the language, they may well find that *Cymry Cymraeg* are eager to switch to English at the earliest opportunity if they find a conversation a struggle.

My vox pop at the National Eisteddfod convinced me that there is a growing awareness of learners' needs among Welsh speakers, but there is still a long way to go. There is a continuing need to educate Welsh speakers on learners' issues. More programmes on Radio Cymru and S4C could help to bring the issue to the forefront of Welsh-speakers' thinking.

Siop Bodlon, Hen Lyfrgell, Cardiff.

Socialising in Hen Lyfrgell.

**Chapter 11**

# Journals and Diaries

## Journals

A learning journal is a compilation of thoughts, reactions and observations about your progress. Writing in an exploratory way may raise self-awareness and self-esteem and, as well, reduce anxiety. Writing can boost a learner's immune system. Nowadays reflecting on learning is a common activity for students studying languages and many other disciplines.

Interestingly, when I used journal writing as part of a research project, several learners told me that, though the main purpose of writing their journals was to help me (the researcher) understand more about how language learners think, it also helped them to change their attitudes. Until they recorded their experiences in their journals, they were unaware of how many practice opportunities they had missed, sometimes because of anxiety.

It would be good to consider writing a journal just for your own benefit. Record any practice opportunities you have for Welsh. You could write about your experiences in class too if you have time. Don't spend too long on this activity. Write your reflections in your first language. You could include reactions to Welsh television programmes, books or magazines you read. How much you write is up to you. Sometimes you will have more to say than at other times.

Every week review what you have written and see if it helps you to identify why you reacted in a certain way, why you missed a practice opportunity, or why you were encouraged or discouraged by encounters with first-language Welsh speakers or other learners. You may like to discuss these matters with your tutor, fellow students or

Welsh speakers you know who speak to you in Welsh. You may just like to reflect on your observations and use them in a constructive way to help you make the most of your learning and practising opportunities.

Keep a notebook for this purpose and always record the date, including the year, so that in the future you can look back and see how your attitudes, confidence and abilities have changed.

## Diaries

At the back of the notebook keep a diary in Welsh. Again, remember to include the date and year. The purpose of the diary is to ensure that, even if it is only for a few minutes, you will be exposed to some Welsh every day and keep your Welsh ticking over, even at times when you cannot attend class or are unable to meet your mentor or any other Welsh speaker.

Write at least one sentence each day. For beginners this may be a very simple sentence, such as *Dw i'n hoffi bwyta pizza* (I like eating pizza). Early on in the learning process you will learn to talk about the past, so each day you could write one sentence about something you have done, such as *Es i i'r gwaith am wyth o'r gloch* (I went to work at eight o'clock) or *Es i i'r sinema i weld y ffilm am Paddington gyda'r plant* (I went to the cinema to see the film about Paddington with the children). Intermediate and advanced learners could write as much as time permits, perhaps summarising a television programme or writing a short book review. You might even like to try writing a *stori fer* (short story).

Alternatively, you could buy a Welsh-language diary and write some Welsh in it each day. Pocket and desk versions are available from Welsh bookshops or direct from the Gwales website or Y Lolfa publishers.

If possible, get your tutor or another fluent speaker to check out your diary occasionally just in case you are repeating and reinforcing some mistakes.

I would recommend using Moleskine notebooks. You can buy a

pack in Waterstones. These are small enough to keep with you at all times. If you write a great deal you can label your *cyfnodolyn/dyddiadur* (journal/diary) when you move on to the next book. It would be good to keep it with your vocabulary book so that they are always to hand when you have a free moment.

Some students may prefer to keep their vocabulary on a smartphone or tablet. This is fine as long as you have it with you to use when there is lull in whatever you are doing. The journal/diary entries and the vocabulary entries need not be an extra burden in your life: they can be done on public transport, in waiting rooms, in the kitchen waiting for food to be ready or anywhere when there are a few minutes to spare. Back up your electronic work periodically as it would be disappointing to lose it.

You can find out more about journal research and read my own journal of using German in *Think Without Limits: you CAN speak Welsh* and *Social Context and Fluency in L2 learners: The case of Wales.* Marilyn Lewis, a Welsh learner in New Zealand, has included her reflective diary in English in her book *How to learn foreign languages* (Palgrave Macmillan, 1999) and it is worth reading.

# Chapter 12

# What is fluency?

Students often ask me questions such as, 'When will I be fluent?' or 'How long will it take me to speak Welsh properly?' There is no set answer to this. So much depends on the students' motivation, responsibilities, effort put into learning and practising, background in language learning and many other factors. And, of course, it all depends on how we define fluency.

When a friend recommended Nate Nicholson's book *How to Become Fluent in Any Language in a Few Months*, I was sceptical. I expected another book full of unrealistic promises. However, when I read how Nate defines fluency, I was drawn in. He views fluency as the ability to communicate with native speakers with relative ease but not 100 per cent accuracy, and claims this can be achieved in a few months. Nate knows this from personal experience. Eager to communicate in Mexico, he taught himself Spanish in the few months before his trip by focusing on what was useful to him, not on becoming perfect. For Nate, 'If you can talk with native speakers of your target language about the usual topics you like talking about in your native language, you're fluent.'

I agree that this is possible as long as there is enough investment of time for practice as the learning progresses. Nate also stresses that learners need the right mind-set. They have to believe in what they are doing and strong motivation is needed to keep learners going through frustrating periods.

Fluency, of course, means different things to different people. The important thing is to use what we know as often as possible, build up vocabulary and focus on pronunciation and intonation. The speed with which students achieve the desired degree of fluency will vary from person to person and could be anything from a few months to many years.

Benny Lewis, of *Fluent in 3 Months* fame, admits that many hours of input are needed each day to achieve fluency in three months. Some students won't have the time if they work long hours and have family responsibilities. That is no reason to give up, however. Why worry if it takes you ten years to become fluent? The important thing is to get to the level of fluency you want. Remember the hare and the tortoise: who won the race? Yes, the tortoise of course. I understand that most people who climb Snowdon from the Llanberis path get to the top in between two and three hours, some dynamic people making it in an hour. It took me over five hours. Did it matter? The views at the top are the same however long the ascent took.

So, is it really how quickly we become fluent that matters? No. It is all about sticking at it and getting there eventually.

Some people already know quite a lot of Welsh from the past, either from school or family, but have lost it because of living outside Wales, perhaps, or for other reasons. In a sense we never lose a language we once spoke. Listening, reading and speaking will bring the language back far quicker than is the case for the new learner. Gabriel Wyner suggests watching a lot of television if you want to revive a 'lost' language.

If you want what some would describe as 'real' fluency though, approaching championship level, and to be able to speak about every subject under the sun in Welsh, there will be many struggles, frustrations and pain, but there will also be great rewards at the end of the day.

**Other reading:**

Nate Nicholson, *How to Become Fluent in Any Language in a Few Months* (Createspace, 2014).

# Chapter 13

# Sustaining motivation

'No matter what your "why" is, it has to be strong enough to fire you up and keep you going when you feel frustrated. It's much easier to learn a language when you have a good reason to do it.'

Nate Nicholson

So we now have an awareness of the importance of pronunciation, vocabulary and idioms and know we need to insist on practice opportunities with fluent speakers. We are even plugging away at a journal and a diary. Are we going to keep this up and sustain our motivation?

Whatever your level, but especially if you are beginner, attend a Welsh class if at all possible. The support of the tutor and your fellow students will encourage you. An intensive course is of particular value. It is not practical for many people but if you can attend a course every weekday you will absorb material quickly. If you are on a weekly course at home, try at some point to go on an intensive weekend or full week course. These inspire students and boost confidence.

Delyth Jones made the following comment after a week's session at Nant Gwrtheyrn, a Welsh-language centre in a beautiful setting on the Llŷn Penninsula.

> '*Cyn dod i'r Nant mi faswn i'n rhewi pan oedd pobl yn siarad Cymraeg efo fi. Rŵan dw i ddim yn panico hyd yn oed os oes rhaid i mi ddefnydio tipyn bach o eiriau Saesneg... Dw i ddim yn gallu credu cymaint dw i wedi dysgu.*'

> (Before coming to the Nant I would freeze when people spoke Welsh to me. Now I do not panic even if I have to use a few English words... I cannot believe how much I have learned.) 99

If an intensive course is not practicable, it is still possible to learn by a drip-feed weekly course, but it will take longer. Attending occasional Saturday courses will make quite a difference too. These popular courses mean you make new friends with other Welsh learners and are able to share experiences.

Courses and tutors are not absolutely essential, though. If you live outside Wales or if you are involved in shift work, you may choose to learn via the internet. Some learners have managed to become fluent in Welsh without any classes initially. Learners from the USA, for instance, such as Tim Jilg who taught himself in Ohio and Chris Cope in Minnesota. I have met several students in Cardiff who started learning with the popular site *https://www.saysomethingin.com/welsh* and are making excellent progress. *Cadw Sŵn* pioneered by Colin Jones of Bridgend, a learner himself, is another option. It consists of a printed course book with twenty lessons of audio on DVD and Blu-ray. Pieces of classical music are played to accompany the learning, as this helps some learners relax and absorb the material more easily. Lists of websites offering online Welsh courses are in Appendix VI. Most are free, but some charge a small fee.

As indicated earlier, it is hugely beneficial to belong to a group so that classroom Welsh is practised, either a group who meet to practise speaking, or a group such as a Welsh choir where Welsh is spoken. This is particularly important if you have no family or close friends to practise what you learn in class. A mentor, that one person to support you and speak to you regularly, is also invaluable.

Motivations for learning Welsh vary considerably. You may want to speak your grandparents' language, help your children at school, use Welsh at work, impress the in-laws or chat to friends. It's the

Nant Gwrthyern.
Photo: Nant Gwrtheyrn

Dr Tim Jilg from Ohio, a fluent learner who wrote his PhD thesis in Welsh.

strength of the motivation that is important, not the type. You need a strong WHY.

It's often learners who are very close to fluency who feel the most discouraged. They do not really belong anywhere. They are neither learners nor native speakers. They can become sensitive if they are referred to as learners, if they are corrected or if well-meaning people say, 'You speak well for a learner.' They are crossing the bridge from learner to second-language speaker. Having a strong WHY should prevent them giving up when the going gets tough.

Making a learning plan helps sustain motivation, too. Decide what you would like to achieve in six months' or a year's time. Form a definite resolution. For several years I have been saying in January, 'This year I am going to revive my German.' Through reading Benny Lewis' blog I came to see the reason why I wasn't making much progress. I had not made a specific enough resolution. So this is my plan for this year. I will speak German at every opportunity. I will read one page of German every day on my Kindle which goes everywhere with me, and during the year I will go through the grammar book and revise the constructions and verbs. You may think one page a day isn't much but I know I will keep that up. If I said 'I will read a book a week,' I know that it would be unlikely to be sustained.

Think of your own realistic, specific resolutions for Welsh. The first one has to be that you will speak Welsh at every opportunity. No excuses. Just dive in. Depending on your level you could have other resolutions. For beginners, for instance: I will watch at least one programme on S4C each week with subtitles. I will write one sentence in Welsh in my diary every day. I will listen to Radio Cymru for five minutes each day. I will buy *Lingo Newydd* and work through the sections for beginners over two months.

You make your own specific, realistic resolutions depending on your level and the time you can allocate. It does not have to be on the first of January that you make your resolution but, whenever it is, make a note of it in your journal and check how far you have been able to stick at it after the allotted time. Tell your tutor or another learner about your resolution so that you are motivated to stick at it rather than lose face.

# Chapter 14

# It's over to you

When I asked successful learners and tutors for their top tips for Welsh learners, there was a general consensus that practising and insisting on using Welsh, even when the Welsh speaker turns to English, is the key to success. Using what they know, not worrying about mistakes and mixing with as many Welsh speakers as possible is what successful learners have done. Exposure to 'real' conversations is very important. Listening to Welsh television, radio and CDs, and reading books will help. But exposing yourself to Welsh conversation, relaxing, and enjoying using Welsh is what will develop your speaking skills most effectively.

So if you really mean it when you say, 'I've always wanted to speak Welsh' or 'I'd love to be fluent' or 'I'd love to help my kids with their Welsh homework,' then that is what you have to do.

It's over to you now. There's plenty of advice in this small book to help you towards communicating in Welsh whatever your motivation. It's time to decide where you are going. Are you going to stay as a professional learner, attending classes but only ever mixing with your friends from Welsh class, staying in your comfort zone? Or are you going out into the community to use the Welsh you know, practise it, extend your knowledge and become immersed in Welsh culture, turning a blind eye to those who, for whatever reason, do not help you.

Is this book going up on the shelf with the other self-help books, I wonder? Make your own specific, realistic resolutions today and write them in your notebook before you put this book away. Then, keep at it each day until you reach your desired goal. You'll need to work hard at it. The only place where Success comes before Work is in a dictionary!

If you decide to follow the advice in this book, I'd love to hear from you and help you towards your goal. Please contact me on Narnians@hotmail.co.uk or become a friend of Lynda Pritchard Newcombe on Facebook to let me know how you are getting on.

> ### *Daliwch ati a mwynhewch!*
> (Stick at it and enjoy!)

# Appendices

## Appendix I

### Books for learners

Browse Gwales.com for a full selection

Some recommendations for *Mynediad, Sylfaen, Canolradd* and *Uwch*

### Mynediad (Entrance)

Elin Meek, *Mynediad i Gymru: 1. Dilyn Dwy Afon – Afon Tywi ac Afon Teifi* (Gwasg Gomer, 2008).

Elin Meek, *Mynediad i Gymru: 2. Mynyddoedd Mawr – Eryri a'i Phobl* (Gwasg Gomer, 2008).

Elin Meek, *Mynediad i Gymru: 3. O'r Tir – Byw yn y Wlad* (Gwasg Gomer, 2008).

Carole Bradley, *Mynediad i Gymru: 4. Cip ar y Cymoedd* (Gwasg Gomer, 2008).

### Sylfaen (Foundation)

Lois Arnold, *Sgwp!* (Gwasg Gomer, 2014).

### Canolradd (Intermediate)

Alun Charles, *Cant y Cant* (Gwasg Gomer, 2010).

### Uwch (Higher)

Cyfres Cam at y Cewri

Islwyn Ffowc Elis, *Cysgod y Cryman* (Gwasg Gomer, 2003).

Islwyn Ffowc Elis, *Yn ôl i Leifior* (Gwasg Gomer, 1989).

## Appendix II

### S4C

www.s4c.co.uk/cy/adloniant/dal-ati/

www.s4c.co.uk/cariadatiaith/

www.s4c.co.uk/clic/

**Radio Cymru**

www.bbc.co.uk/podcasts/series/pigion

## Appendix III
### Regional Variations

| *De* South | *Gogledd* North |
| --- | --- |
| Mam-gu (grandmother) | Nain |
| Tad-cu (grandfather) | Taid |
| Gyda (with) | Efo |
| Fe (he) | Fo |
| Llaeth (milk) | Llefrith |
| Allwedd (key) | Agoriad |
| Mae ... gyda fi (I have) | Mae gen i |

## Appendix IV
### Contacts for Socialising and Other Useful Websites

http://www.mentrauiaith.org/

(Mentrau Iaith Cymru – promoting the Welsh language in the community)

**Menter Iaith Abertawe**

01792 460 906 | swyddfa@menterabertawe.org

**Menter Iaith Sir Benfro**

01239 831129 / 01348 873700 | ymholiad@mentersirbenfro.com

**Menter Bro Ogwr**

01656 732200 | menter@broogwr.org

**Menter Brycheiniog a Maesyfed**

08708 510583 | menter.brycheiniog@powys.gov.uk

**Menter Caerdydd**

029 20 689 888 | menter@caerdydd.org

**Menter Iaith Sir Caerffili**

01443 820913 | menter@caerffili.org

**Menter Castell Nedd Port Talbot**

01792 864949 | menter@micnpt.org

**Cered (Menter Ceredigion)**
01545 572350 | cered@ceredigion.gov.uk
**Menter Iaith Sir Ddinbych**
01745 812822 | menter@menterdinbych.org
**Menter Iaith Conwy**
01492 642357 | meirion@miconwy.org
**Menter Iaith Sir Y Fflint**
01352 744040 | gwybod@menteriaithsiryfflint.co.uk
**Menter Iaith Blaenau Gwent Torfaen a Mynwy**
01495 762 446 | menter@menterbgtm.org
**Menter Merthyr Tudful**
01685 722176 | menter@merthyrtudful.com
**Menter Iaith Maelor**
01978 363791 | busnes@menteriaithmaelor.org
**Menter Maldwyn**
01686 614020 | menterm@powys.gov.uk
**Menter Iaith Môn**
01248 725700 | iaith@mentermon.com
**Menter Iaith Rhondda Cynon Taf**
01443 407570 | menter@menteriaith.org
**Menter Bro Dinefwr**
01558 825336 / 01269 596622 | post@menterbrodinefwr.org
**Menter Gorllewin Sir Gâr**
01239 712934 | ymholiad@mentergorllewinsirgar.org.uk
**Menter Cwm Gwendraeth – Llanelli**
01269 871600 / 01554 758355 |
ymholiadau@mentercwmgwendraeth.org.uk
**Menter Iaith Casnewydd**
01633 466017 | elinmaher@menteriaithcasnewydd.org

**www.merchedywawr.co.uk**
(an organisation for women similar to the Women's Institute but all
communication is in Welsh)

**www.cymdeithasedwardllwyd.org.uk**

http://www.southwales.ac.uk/cymraeg/cyfleoedd-cymraeg/cymdeithasu-yn-y-gymraeg/

www.londonwelsh.org/learn-welsh

http://www.cymdeithas.org.uk/

**www.welshforadults.org**
(to find a course in your area)

**www.nantgwrtheyrn.org**
(Welsh language and heritage centre at Nant Gwrtheyrn)

**www.ybont.org**
(a national Welsh for Adults e-learning platform)

**www.acen.co.uk**
(language and resources centre for Welsh learners)

**www.urdd.org**
(a national organisation for children and young people)

**www.eisteddfod.org.uk**
(the National Eisteddfod for Wales)

**www.twfcymru.com**
(information and advice on raising children bilingually)

**www.mym.co.uk**
(Mudiad Meithrin, the Welsh early years' specialists)

## Appendix V
### *Cyngor i Gymry Cymraeg – Beth allech chi wneud i helpu?*
- *Cymerwch bob cyfle i ddefnyddio Cymraeg gyda dysgwyr.*
- *Os oes dysgwyr yn aelod o'ch clwb/cymdeithas chi, gwnewch bwynt o gael sgwrs o leiaf pum munud gyda nhw bob wythnos er mwyn eu helpu nhw i wella.*
- *Os ydych yn aelod o glwb/cymdeithas neu fudiad Cymraeg, pam na wnewch chi drefnu digwyddiad ar y cyd gyda Chanolfan Cymraeg i Oedolion?*
- *Beth am wahodd dysgwr rydych chi'n adnabod i fynychu gyda chi i gael blas o'ch gweithgaredd?*

- Beth am drefnu i fod yn siaradwr gwadd mewn dosbarth neu glwb i ddysgwyr?
- Beth am ymweld â Maes D yn ystod yr Eisteddfod Genedlaethol i gael sgwrs gyda nifer o ddysgwyr yno?
- Mae nifer fawr o weithgareddau yn cael eu trefnu ar gyfer dysgwyr dros Gymru drwy'r flwyddyn. Cysylltwch â'r darparwyr yn eich ardal chi i weld beth dych chi'n gallu gwneud i helpu dysgwyr.

### Sut mae siarad â dysgwyr:

- Gwrandwch yn astud.
- Anogwch ddysgwyr i siarad Cymraeg bob amser.
- Siaradwch yn glir heb fod yn nawddoglyd.
- Dechreuwch bob sgwrs yn Gymraeg.
- Gadewch iddyn nhw droi i'r Saesneg pan fyddan nhw'n cael trafferthion – OND parhewch chi i siarad Cymraeg. Gwnaiff y dysgwr droi yn ôl i'r Gymraeg yn y pen draw.
- Dewiswch eich geiriau'n ofalus.
- Cynyddwch yr amser rydych yn siarad Cymraeg â dysgwyr yn eich teulu bob wythnos.
- Byddwch yn gyfeillgar.
- Byddwch yn amyneddgar.
- Os oes partner gyda chi sy'n dysgu, anogwch nhw i ddefnyddio ymadrodd ychwanegol gyda'r plant bob wythnos.

### Triwch beidio:

- Defnyddio iaith gymhleth.
- Gorffen brawddeg ar eu rhan, na thorri ar draws.
- Chwerthin.
- Bod yn negyddol, na nawddoglyd.
- Troi'r sgwrs i'r Saesneg os nad yw'r dysgwr wedi deall rhywbeth – esboniwch ystyr y frawddeg yn Saesneg ac wedyn trowch yn ôl i'r Gymraeg.
- Siarad yn rhy gyflym gan ddefnyddio iaith dafodieithol.
- Dweud "We don't say it like that."

- *Siarad Saesneg.*
- *Cywiro eu hiaith (os nad ydyn nhw'n gofyn).*
- *Rhoi gwers ramadeg iddyn nhw – swydd y tiwtor yw hynny.*

**Advice to Welsh speakers – What can you do to help?**
- Take every opportunity to use Welsh with learners.
- If learners are members of your club/society, make a point of having a chat with them for at least five minutes every week to help them to improve.
- If you are a member of a club/society or a Welsh movement, why don't you arrange a joint event with a centre where adults learn Welsh?
- What about inviting learners you know to attend and to get a taste for the activity?
- What about arranging to be a guest speaker in a class or a learners' club?
- What about visiting Maes D during the National Eisteddod to have a chat with some of the learners there?
- There are many activities for learners arranged in Wales throughout the year. Contact your local providers so see what you can do to help learners.

**How to speak to learners:**
- Listen carefully.
- Always encourage learners to speak.
- Speak clearly but do not be condescending.
- Start every conversation in Welsh.
- Let them turn to English when they have problems – BUT continue to speak in Welsh. The learners will turn back to Welsh eventually.
- Choose your words carefully.
- Increase the time you speak to learners in your family each week.
- Be friendly.

- Be patient.
- If you have a partner who is learning, encourage them to use a new expression with the children every week.

**Try not to:**
- Use complicated language.
- Finish a sentence for them or interrupt them.
- Laugh.
- Be negative or condescending.
- Turn to English if the learner has not understood something – explain the meaning of the sentence in English and then turn to Welsh.
- Speak too quickly using dialect.
- Say "We don't say it like that."
- Speak English.
- Correct their language (unless they ask).
- Give them a grammar lesson – this is the role of the tutor.

## Appendix VI

Online Welsh lessons

http://www.saysomethinginwelsh.com

https://www.duolingo.com/course/cy/en/Learn-Welsh-Online

http://www.bbc.co.uk/learnwelsh/

http://www.bbc.co.uk/colinandcumberland/

http://www.s4c.co.uk/dysgwyr/

http://www.cs.brown.edu/fun/welsh/Welsh.html

# Acknowledgements

My heartfelt thanks go to all the learners, tutors and first-language Welsh speakers who have shared their thoughts and experiences with me. You are too many to list here but please be assured of my sincere appreciation. Without you this book would not have been written.

Special thanks to Professor Viv Edwards of Reading University who read a first draft of the early chapters and gave encouraging and constructive comments. Many thanks to Gwenllian Willis of Cardiff University who read the completed book and suggested some useful additions.

I would also like to thank my husband, Robert, for his support and conscientious proof-reading and of course Lefi Gruffudd and Elin Angharad of Y Lolfa for their interest in the manuscript.

My special thanks to Eirian Jones for her hard work editing the book.

# Also by the Author

*Social Context and Fluency in L2 Learners:  The Case of Wales*

*Think Without Limits: you CAN speak Welsh*